D1602466

# CHARLES H. SPURGEON

# SPURGEON

## *The Best from All His Works*

# OTHER AUTHORS IN THE SERIES

George MacDonald: The Best from All His Works

F. B. Meyer: The Best from All His Works

Andrew Murray: The Best from All His Works

# CHARLES H. SPURGEON

## The Best from All His Works

by
Charles H. Spurgeon
*Abridged and edited by Charles Erlandson*

THE
CHRISTIAN
CLASSICS
COLLECTION

**THOMAS NELSON PUBLISHERS**
Nashville

Published in Nashville, Tennessee, by Thomas Nelson, Inc. and distributed in Canada by Lawson Falle, Ltd., Cambridge, Ontario.

Printed in the United States of America.

*Scripture quotations are from the King James Version of the Bible.*

**Library of Congress Cataloging-in-Publication Data**

Spurgeon, C. H. (Charles Haddon), 1834–1892.
   [Selections. 1988]
   Charles H. Spurgeon, the best from all his works / Charles H. Spurgeon ; abridged and edited by Charles Erlandson.
      p.   cm.—(The Christian classics collection ; vol. 5)
   ISBN 0-8407-7441-9
   1. Spiritual life.  I. Erlandson, Charles.  II. Title.
III. Series.
BV4501.S822   1988
252'.061—dc19                       88–22396
                                        CIP

1 2 3 4 5 6 — 93 92 91 90 89 88

# Contents

**CHARLES H. SPURGEON**

Charles Haddon Spurgeon was born on June 19, 1834, in Kelvedon in Essex County, England. Raised in a Christian home, he nevertheless experienced a season of doubt which ended in a dramatic conversion in 1849. In 1851 the seventeen-year-old Spurgeon obtained his first regular pastorate. Everywhere he preached throughout his life, enthusiastic crowds thronged to hear him, and on one occasion he preached to a gathering of 23,654. His dynamic, theological, and mellifluous sermons led those who heard him to call him "The Prince of Preachers."

On March 31, 1861, the first Sunday service was held in Spurgeon's Metropolitan Tabernacle. Built to accommodate up to six thousand of Spurgeon's crowds, it was still never large enough to contain those who wanted to hear him. Spurgeon's ministry in the Metropolitan Tabernacle was known not only for his electrifying sermons but also for its Christian service. As great as his influence was through his preaching, it may have been even greater through the many young pastors he trained in his Pastor's College. He was also responsible for establishing an almshouse and an orphanage. Altogether, there were sixty-six Spurgeonic institutions. In addition to his sermons, which he revised and published weekly and which sold extremely well, he also began publishing a monthly magazine, *The Sword and Trowel,* in 1865.

Spurgeon suffered from gout for most of his life and was in chronically poor health after 1867. He died January 31, 1892, leaving a legacy of written material that continues to exert a tremendous influence on believers throughout the world.

# Introduction

It is virtually impossible to winnow the best of Spurgeon's written work down to the size of one volume. His output was simply enormous. He was interested in books from a very early age, and even at the age of fifteen he was prolific, writing a two hundred ninety-five-page essay titled *Popery Unmasked*. His printed sermons occupy sixty-two volumes of four hundred eighty small-print pages each, and in addition to his sermons he published one hundred forty works during his lifetime.

When the name Spurgeon is mentioned, his sermons immediately come to mind. Many reasons have been given for the greatness of those works. For example, Spurgeon was always theologically oriented, and the most profound truths of the Christian doctrine are illuminated in his sermons. In particular, he strongly defended Calvinistic theology in all of its splendor.

But Spurgeon's sermons are far from dry: Their simplicity is refreshing and reaches all men. Spurgeon's sermons also strike one as being vital and earnest. They are close to life and Spurgeon's faith genuinely touched to the depths of his soul. Finally, Spurgeon always had the welfare of his audience in mind, and there is a persistent evangelistic tone in his sermons.

Spurgeon's other works are also worthy of mention. His *Treasury of David* is widely regarded as one of the best commentaries ever written on the Psalms. *Lectures to My Students* is read by pastors today, and his works on grace are considered classics on that topic. Perhaps it is presumptuous to call any collection "The Best of Spurgeon," but after reading a volume of Spurgeon's works one might be convinced that that is exactly what he has just read.

# CHARLES H. SPURGEON

## The Best from All His Works

The first sermon selected for this volume, "Grace Abounding over Abounding Sin," was delivered on March 4, 1888, at the Metropolitan Tabernacle. In it, Spurgeon expounds one of his favorite themes throughout his sermons and his other works: grace. Spurgeon finds that if we want to see where God's grace abounds we need only look at where men have sinned most. Like many of Spurgeon's sermons, "Grace Abounding over Abounding Sin" concludes with an appeal to sinners to accept this grace.

1888, the year "Grace Abounding over Abounding Sin" was given, found Spurgeon engaged in the Down-Grade Controversy, the most bitter controversy of his life. Keenly aware of the apostasy of the times and the increasing strength of those in the church who denied the full authority of Scripture, Spurgeon published several articles in The Sword and the Trowel urging those of faith to dissociate themselves from such men. It was from the title of the first of these that the controversy received its name. Eventually, as a result of the controversy this provoked and the feelings that ran contrary to his own, Spurgeon left the Baptist Union. Many of Spurgeon's sermons of 1887 and 1888 reflect the Down-Grade Controversy, and the pain it brought to him.

## CHAPTER ONE

# Grace Abounding over Abounding Sin

*Moreover the law entered, that the offense might abound. But where sin abounded, grace did much more abound (Rom. 5:20).*

The first sentence will serve as a preface; the second sentence will be the actual text.

## The Law and Abounding Offense

"Moreover the law entered, that the offense might abound." Man was a sinner before the law of Ten Commandments had been given. He was a sinner through the offence of his first father, Adam; and he was, also, practically a sinner by his own personal offense; for he rebelled against the light of nature, and the inner light of conscience. Men, from Adam downward, transgressed against that memory of better days which had been handed down from father to son, and had never been quite forgotten. Man everywhere, whether he knew anything about the law of Moses or not, was alienated from his God. The Word of God contains this truthful estimate of our race: "They are all gone out of the way, they are together become unprofitable; there is none that doeth good, no, not one."

The law was given, however, according to the text, "that the offense might abound." Such was the effect of the law. It did not hinder sin, nor provide a remedy for it; but its actual effect was that the offence abounded. How so?

It was so, first, because it revealed the offense. Man did not in every instance clearly discern what was sin; but when the law came, it pointed out to man that this evil, which he thought little of, was an abomination in the sight of God. Man's nature and character was like a dark dungeon which knew no ray of light. Yonder prisoner does not perceive the horrible filthiness and corruption of the place wherein he is immured, so long as he is in darkness. When a lamp is brought, or a window is opened and the light of day comes in, he finds out to his dismay the hideous condition of his den. He spies loathsome creatures upon the walls, and marks how others burrow out of sight because the light annoys them. He may, perhaps, have guessed that all was not as it should be, but he had not imagined the abundance of the evils. The light has entered, and the offense abounds.

Law does not make us sinful, but it displays our sinfulness. In the presence of the perfect standard we see our shortcomings. The law of God is the looking-glass in which a man sees the spots upon his face. It does not wash you—you cannot wash in a looking-glass; but it prompts you to seek the cleansing water. The design of the law is the revealing of our many offenses, that, thereby, we may be driven out of self-righteousness to the Lord Jesus, in whom we have redemption through his blood, the forgiveness of sin.

The law causes the offense to abound by making an offender to stand without excuse. Before he knew the law perfectly, his sin was not so wilful. While he did but faintly know the commands, he could, as it were, but faintly break them; but as soon as he distinctly knows what is right, and what is wrong, then every cloak is taken away from him. Sin becomes exceeding sinful when it is committed against light and knowledge. Is it not so with some of you? Are you not forced to admit that you commit many sins in one, now that you have been made to know the law, and yet wilfully offend against it, by omission or commission? He who knows his Master's will and does it not, will be beaten with many stripes, because he is guilty of abounding offenses. The law enters to strip us of every cloak of justification, and so to drive us to seek the robe of Christ's righteousness.

Next, I think the law makes the offense to abound by causing sin to be, more evidently, a presumptuous rebellion against the great Lawgiver. To sin in the front of Sinai, with its wonderful display of divine majesty, is to sin indeed. To rebel against a law promulgated with sound of trumpet, and thunders, and pomp of God, is to sin with a high hand and a defiant heart. When thou hast heard the Ten Commands, when thou knowest the law of the kingdom, when thy Maker's will is plainly set before thee, then to transgress is to transgress with an insolence of pride which will admit of no excuse.

Once more: the entrance of the law makes the offense to abound in this sense, that the rebellious will of man rises up in opposition to it. Because God commands, man refuses; and because he forbids, man desires. There are some men who might not have sinned in a particular direction if the commandment had not forbidden it. The light of the law, instead of being a warning to them to avoid evil, seems to point out to them the way in which they can most offend.

Oh, how deep is the depravity of human nature! The law itself provokes it to rebel. Men long to enter, because trespassers are warned to keep away. Their minds are so at enmity against God, that they delight in that which is forbidden, not so much because they find any particular pleasure in the thing itself, but because it shows their independence and their freedom from the restraints of God. This vicious self-will is in all of us by nature; for the carnal mind is enmity against God; and therefore the law, though in itself holy and just and good, provokes us to do evil. We are like lime, and the law is as cold water, which is in itself of a cooling nature; yet, no sooner does the water of the law get at the lime of our nature, than a heat of sin is generated: "thus, the law entered, that the offense might abound."

## The Use of the Law

Why, then, did God send the law? Is it not an evil thing that the offense should abound? In itself it may seem so to be; but God dealeth with us as physicians sometimes deal with their patients. A disease, which will be fatal if it spends itself within the patient, must be brought to the surface: the physician therefore prescribes a medicine which displays the evil. The evil was all within, but it did not abound as to its visible effects; it is needful that it should do so, that it may be cured.

The law is the medicine which throws out the depravity of man, makes him see it in his actions, and even provokes him to display it. The evil is in man, like rabbits in yonder brushwood: the law sets alight to the cover, and the hidden creatures are seen. The law stirs the mud at the bottom of the pool, and proves how foul the waters are. The law compels the man to see that sin dwelleth in him, and that it is a powerful tyrant over his nature. All this is with a view to his cure. God be thanked when the law so works as to take off the sinner from all confidence in himself! To make the leper confess that he is incurable is going a great way towards compelling him to go to that Divine Savior, who alone is able to heal him. This is the object and end of the law towards men whom God will save.

Consider for a moment. You may take it as an axiom, a thing self-evident, that there can be no grace where there is no guilt: there can be no mercy where there is no sin. There can be justice, there can be benevolence; but there cannot be mercy unless there is criminality. If you are not a sinner God cannot have mercy upon you. If you have never sinned God cannot display pardoning grace towards you, for there is nothing to pardon. It were a misuse of words to talk of forgiving a man who has done no wrong, or to speak of bestowing undeserved favor upon a person who deserves reward. It would be an insult to innocence to offer it mercy. You must, therefore, have sin or you cannot have grace—that is clear.

Next, consider that there will be no seeking after grace where there is no sense of sin. We may preach till we are hoarse, but you good people, who have never broken the law, and are not guilty of anything wrong, will never care for our message of mercy. You are such kind people that, out of compliment to religion, you say, "Yes, we are sinners. We are all sinners." But you know in your heart of hearts you do not mean it. You will never ask for grace; for you have no sense of shame or guilt. None of you will seek mercy, till first you have pleaded guilty to the indictment which the law of God presents against you. Oh, that you felt your sins! Oh, that you knew your need of forgiveness! for then you would see yourselves to be in such a condition that only the free, rich, sovereign grace of God can save you.

Furthermore, I am sure that there will be no reception and acceptance of grace by any man, till there is a full confession of sin and a burdensome sense of its weight. Why should you receive grace when you do not want it? What is the use of it to you? Why should you bow your knee to God, and receive, as the free gift of his charity, that which you feel you deserve? Have you not already earned eternal life? Are you not as good as other people? Have you not some considerable claim upon God? Do I startle you with these plain questions? Have I not heard you say much the same?

The other day when we preached the electing love of God, you grumbled and muttered that God was unjust to choose one rather than another. What did this mean? Did it not mean that you felt you had some claim upon God? O sir, if this is your spirit, I must deal plainly with you! If you have any claim upon your Maker, plead it, and be you sure that he will not deny you your just rights. But I would advise you to change your method of dealing with your Judge: you will never prevail in this fashion. In truth, you have no claim upon him; but must appeal to his pure mercy. You are not in a position for him to display free grace to you till your mouth is shut, and you sit down in dust and ashes, silently owning that you deserve nothing at his hands but infinite displeasure. Confess that whatever he gives you that is good and gracious must be given freely to one who deserves nothing. Hell gapes at your feet: cease from pride, and humbly sue out a pardon.

You see, then, the use of the law: it is to bring you where grace can be fitly shown you. It shuts you up that you may cry to Jesus to set you free. It is a storm which wrecks your hopes of self-salvation, but washes you upon the Rock of Ages. The condemning sentence of the law is meant to prepare you for the absolution of the gospel. If you condemn yourself and plead guilty before God, the royal pardon can then be extended towards you. The self-condemned shall be forgiven through the precious blood of Jesus, and the sovereign grace of God.

Oh, my hearer, you must sit down there in the dust, or else God will not look at you! You must yield yourself to him, owning his justice, honoring his law: this is the first condition of his mercy, and to this his grace brings all who feel its power. The Lord will have you bow before him in self-abhorrence, and confess his right to punish you. Remember, "He will have mercy on whom he will have mercy, and he will have compassion on whom he will have compassion," and he will have you know this, and agree to it. His grace must reign triumphantly, and you must kiss its silver scepter.

Thus has the first sentence served us for a preface: God bless it to us!

## Grace over Sin

The doctrine of the text itself is this, that "where sin abounded, grace did much more abound"; and I shall try to bring out that truth, first, by saying that THIS IS SEEN IN THE WHOLE WORK OF GRACE, from beginning to end.

I would direct your attention to the context. The safest way to preach upon a text, is to follow out the idea which the inspired writer was endeavoring to convey. Paul has, in this place, been speaking of the abounding result for evil of one sin in the case of Adam, the federal head of the race. That one sin of Adam's abounded terribly. Look at the multitudinous generations of our race which have gone down to death. Who slew all these? Sin is the wolf which has devoured the flocks of men. Sin has poisoned the streams of manhood at their fountain-head, and everywhere they run with poisoned waters. Concerning this, Paul says, "Where sin abounded, grace did much more abound."

First, then, *sin abounded in its effect upon the whole human race:* one sin overthrew all humanity; one fatal fault, the breach of a plain and easy law, made sinners of us all. "By one man's disobedience many were made sinners." Simple as was the command which Adam broke, it involved obedience or disobedience to the sovereignty of God. All the trees of the garden were generously given to happy Adam in Paradise: "Of every tree of the garden thou mayest freely eat." There was but one tree reserved for God by the prohibition, "Thou shalt not eat of it: for in the day that thou eatest thereof thou shalt surely die." Adam had no need to touch that fruit, there were all the other trees for him. Nothing was denied him which was really for his good; he was only forbidden that which would ruin him. We all look back to that Paradisaical state and wish we could have been put in some such a position as he: yet he dared to trespass on God's reserves, and thus to set himself up above his Maker. He judged it wise to do what God forbade: he ran the risk of death in the foolish hope of rising into a still higher state.

See the consequences of that sin on all sides, the world is full of them. Yet, saith Paul, "Where sin abounded, grace did much more abound," and he gives us this as a proof of it: "And not as it was by one that sinned, so is the gift: for the judgment was by one to condemnation,

but the free gift is of many offenses unto justification"
(Rom. 5:16). The Lord Jesus came into the world, not
alone to put away Adam's sin, but all the sins which have
followed upon it. The second Adam has repaired the desperate ruin of the first, and much more. By his death
upon the cross, our Divine Substitute has put away those
myriads of sins, which have been committed by men
since the first offense in Eden.

Think of this! Take the whole aggregate of believers,
and let each one disburden his conscience of its load of
sin. What a mountain! Pile it up! Pile it up! It rises huge
as high Olympus! Age after age believers come and lay
their enormous loads in this place. "The Lord hath made
to meet on him the iniquities of us all." What Alps! What
Himalayas of sin! If there were only mine and yours, my
brother, what mountains of division would our sins
make! But the great Christ, the free gift of God to us,
when he bare our sins in his own body on the tree, took
all those countless sins away. "Behold the Lamb of God,
which taketh away the sin of the world"! Here is infinite
grace to pardon immeasurable sin! Truly the "one man's
offense" abounded horribly; but the "one man's obedience," the obedience of the Son of God, hath super-
abounded. As the arch of heaven far exceedeth in its
span the whole round globe of the earth, so doth grace
much more abound over human sin.

Follow me further, when I notice, secondly, that *sin
abounded in its ruinous effects*. It utterly destroyed humanity. In the third chapter of the Romans you see how,
in every part of his nature, man is depraved by sin. Think
of the havoc which the tyrant, sin, has made of our natural estate and heritage. Eden is withered—its very site is
forgotten. Our restfulness among the trees of the field,
freely yielding their fruit, is gone, and God hath said, "In

the sweat of thy face shalt thou eat bread." The field we till has lost its spontaneous yield of corn: "Thorns also and thistles shall it bring forth to thee." Our life has lost its glory and immortality; for "Dust thou art, and unto dust shalt thou return." Every woman in her pangs of travail, every man in his weariness of labor, and all of us together in the griefs of death, see what sin has done for us as to our mortal bodies.

Alas, it has gone deeper: it has ruined our souls. Sin has unmanned man. The crown and glory of his manhood it has thrown to the ground. All our faculties are out of gear; all our tendencies are perverted. Beloved, let us rejoice that the Lord Jesus Christ has come to redeem us from the curse of sin, and he will undo the evil of evil. Even this poor world he will deliver from the bondage of corruption; and he will create new heavens and a new earth, wherein dwelleth righteousness. The groans and painful travail of the whole creation shall result in a full deliverance, through the grace of our Lord Jesus Christ, and somewhat more.

As for ourselves, we are lifted up to a position far higher than that which we should have occupied had the race continued in its innocence. The Lord Jesus Christ found us in a horrible pit and in the miry clay, and he not only lifted us up out of it, but he set our feet upon a rock, and established our goings. Raised from hell, we are lifted not to the bowers of Eden, but to the throne of God. Redeemed human nature has greater capacities than unfallen human nature. To Adam the Lord did not say, "Thou art a son of God, joint heir with the Only-Begotten"; but he has said that to each believer redeemed by the precious blood of Jesus. Beloved, such a thing as fellowship with Christ in his sufferings could not have been known to Adam in Paradise. He could not have known what it is to be dead, and to have his life hid with Christ in God.

Blessed be his name, our Lord Jesus Christ can say, "I restored that which I took away"! He restored more than ever was taken away from us; for he hath made us to be partakers of the divine nature, and in his own person he hath placed us at God's right hand in the heavenly places. Inasmuch as the dominion of the Lord Jesus is more glorious than that of unfallen Adam, manhood is now more great and glorious than before the Fall. Grace has so much more abounded, that in Jesus we have gained more than in Adam we lost. Our Paradise Regained is far more glorious than our Paradise Lost.

Again, *sin abounded to the dishonor of God*. I was trying the other day to put myself into the position of Satan at the gates of Eden, that I might understand his diabolical policy. He had become the archenemy of God, and when he saw this newly-made world, and perceived two perfectly pure and happy creatures placed in it, he looked on with envy, and plotted mischief. He heard the Creator say, "In the day that thou eatest thereof thou shalt surely die," and he hoped here to find an opportunity for an assault upon God. If he could induce those new-made creatures to eat of the forbidden fruit, he would place their Maker upon the horns of a dilemma: either he must destroy the creatures which he had made, or else he must be untrue. The Lord had said, "Ye shall surely die," and he must thus undo his own work, and destroy a creature which he had made in his own image, after his own likeness.

Satan, probably, perceived that man was an extraordinary being, with a wonderful mystery of glory hanging about his destiny; and, if he could make him sin, he would cause God to destroy him, and so far defeat the eternal purpose. On the other hand, if the Lord did not execute the sentence, then he would not be truthful, and throughout all his great universe it would be reported that the Lord's word had been broken. Either he had changed his mind, or he had spoken in jest, or he had been proven to have threatened too severe a penalty. In either case, the evil spirit hoped to triumph. It was a deep, far-reaching scheme to dim the splendor of the King of kings.

Beloved, did it not seem as if sin had abounded beyond measure, when first the woman and then the man had been deceived, and had done despite to God? Behold how grace, through our Lord Jesus Christ, did much more abound! God is more honored in the redemption of man than if there had never been a Fall. The Lord has displayed the majesty of his justice, and the glory of his grace, in the great sacrifice of his dear Son, in such a manner that angels, and principalities, and powers will wonder throughout all ages. More of God is to be seen in the great work of redeeming love than could have been reflected in the creation of myriads of worlds, had each one of them been replete with marvels of divine skill, and goodness, and power. In Jesus crucified Jehovah is glorified as never before. Where sin abounded to the apparent dishonor of God, grace doth much more abound to the infinite glory of his ever-blessed name.

Again, *sin abounded by degrading human character.* What a wretched being man is, as a sinner against God! Unchecked by law, and allowed to do as he pleases, what will not man become? See how Paul describes men in these progressive times—in these enlightened centuries: "This know also, that in the last days perilous times shall come. For men shall be lovers of their own selves, covetous, boasters, proud, blasphemers, disobedient to parents, unthankful, unholy, without natural affection, trucebreakers, false accusers, incontinent, fierce, despisers of those that are good, traitors, heady, high-minded, lovers of pleasures more than lovers of God; having a form of godliness, but denying the power thereof."

Human nature was not at all slandered by Whitefield when he said that, "left to himself, man is half beast and half devil." I do not mean merely men in savage countries, I am thinking of men in London. Only the other day a certain newspaper gave us plenty of proof of the sin of this city: I will say no more—could brutes or demons be worse? Read human history, Assyrian, Roman, Greek, Saracenic, Spanish, English; and if you are a lover of holiness, you will be sick of man. Has any other creature, except the fallen angels, ever become so cruel, so mean, so false? Behold what villains, what tyrants, what monsters sin has made!

But now look on the other side, and see what the grace of God has done. Under the molding hand of the Holy Spirit a gracious man becomes the noblest work of God. Man, born again and rescued from the Fall, is now capable of virtues, to which he never could have reached before he sinned. An unfallen being could not hate sin with the intensity of abhorrence which is found in the renewed heart. We now know by personal experience the horror of sin, and there is now within us an instinctive shuddering at it. An unfallen being could not exhibit patience, for it could not suffer, and patience has its perfect work to do. When I have read the stories of the martyrs in the first ages of the Christian church, and during the Marian persecution in England, I have adored the Lord, who could enable poor feeble men and women thus to prove their love to their God and Savior. What great things they suffered out of love to God; and how grandly did they thus honor him!

O God, what a noble being thy grace has made man to be! I have felt great reverence for sanctified humanity, when I have seen how men could sing God's praises in the fires. What noble deeds men have been capable of, when the love of God has been shed abroad in their hearts! I do not think angels, or archangels, have ever been able to exhibit so admirable an all-round character as the grace of God hath wrought in once fallen men whom he has, by his grace, inspired with the divine life. In human character, "where sin abounded, grace did much more abound." I believe God looks out of heaven to-day, and sees in many of his poor, hidden people such beauties of virtue, such charms of holiness, that he himself is delighted with them. "The Lord taketh pleasure in them that fear him." These are such true jewels that the Lord has a high estimate of them, and sets them apart for himself: "They shall be mine, saith the Lord of hosts, in that day when I make up my jewels."

Again, dear friends, *sin abounded to the causing of great sorrow*. It brought with it a long train of woes. The children of sin are many, and each one causeth lamentation. We cannot attempt to fathom the dark abysses of sorrow which have opened in this world since the advent of sin. Is it not a place of tears—yea, a field of blood? Yet by a wonderful alchemy, through the existence of sin, grace has produced a new joy, yea, more than one new joy. The calm, deep joy of repentance must have been unknown to perfect innocence. This right orient pearl is not found in the rivers of Eden. Yea, and that joy which is in heaven in the presence of the angels of God over sinners that repent is a new thing, whose birth is since the Fall.

God himself knows a joy which he could not have

known had there been no sin. Behold, with tearful wonder, the great Father as he receives his returning prodigal, and cries to all about him, "Let us eat, and be merry: for this my son was dead, and is alive again; he was lost, and is found." O brethren, how could almighty love have been victorious in grace had there been no sin to battle with? Heaven is the more heaven for us, since there we shall sing of robes washed white in the blood of the Lamb. God hath greater joy in man, and man hath greater joy in God, because grace abounded over sin. We are getting into deep waters now! How true our text is!

Once more, *sin abounded to hinder the reign of Christ*. I believe that Satan's design in leading men into sin at the first, was to prevent the supremacy of the Lord Jesus Christ as man and God in one person. I do not lay it down as a doctrine, specifically taught in Scripture, but still it seems to me a probable truth, that Satan foresaw that the gap which was made in heaven by the fall of the angels was to be filled up by human beings, whom God would place near his throne. Satan thought that he saw before him the beings who would take the places of the fallen spirits, and he envied them. He knew that they were made in the image of the Only-Begotten, the Christ of God, and he hated him because he saw united in his person God whom he abhorred, and man whom he envied.

Satan shot at the second Adam through the breast of the first Adam. He meant to overthrow the Coming One; but, fool that he was, the Lord Jesus Christ, by the grace of God, is now exalted higher than ever we could conceive him to have been, had there been no sin to bear, no redemption to work out. Jesus, wounded and slain, has about him higher splendor than before. O Kings of kings and Lord of lords, Man of Sorrows, we sing hallelujahs unto thee! All our hearts beat true to thee! We love thee beyond all else! Thou art he whom we will praise for ever and ever! Jesus sits on no precarious throne in the empire of love. We would each one maintain his right with the last pulse of our hearts. King of kings and Lord of lords! Hallelujah! Where sin abounded, grace hath much more abounded to the glory of the Only-Begotten Son of God.

## Grace over Sin in Special Cases

I find time always flies fastest when our subject is most precious. I have a second head, which deserves a lengthened consideration; but we must be content with mere hints. This great fact, that where sin abounded, grace did much more abound, crops up everywhere. THIS IS TO BE SEEN IN SPECIAL CASES.

The first special case is *the introduction of the law.* When the law of Ten Commands was given, through man's sin, it ministered to the abounding of the offense; but it also ministered to the aboundings of grace. It is true there were ten commands; but there was more than tenfold grace. With the law there came forward a High Priest. The world had never seen a High Priest before, arrayed in jewelled breastplate, and garments of glory and beauty. There was the law; but at the same time there was the holy place of the Tabernacle of the Most High with its altar, its laver, its candlestick, and its table of shew-bread. There was, also, the secret shrine where the majesty of God dwelt. God had, by those symbols and types, come to dwell among men.

It is true, sin abounded through the law; but, then, sacrifices for sin also abounded. Heretofore, there had been no morning and evening lambs; there had been no day of atonement; no sprinkling of blood; no benediction from the Lord's High Priest. For every sin that the law revealed, a sacrifice was provided. Sins of ignorance, sins of their holy things, sins of all sorts were met by special sacrifices; so that the sins uncovered to the conscience, were also covered by the sacrifice.

*The story of Israel* is another case in point. How often the nation rebelled; but how often did mercy rejoice over judgment! Truly the history of the chosen people shows how sin abounded, and grace did much more abound.

Run your eye down history and pause at *the crucifixion of our Lord Jesus.* This is the highest peak of the mountains of sin. They crucified the Lord of glory. Here sin abounded. But do I need to tell you that grace did here much more abound? You can look at the death of Christ till Pilate vanishes, and Caiaphas fades away, and all the clamor of the priests and Jews is hushed, and you see nothing and hear nothing but free grace and dying love.

There followed upon the crucifixion of our Lord, *the casting away of the Jewish people for a while.* Sin abounded when the Lord thus came to his own and his own received him not. Yes; but the casting away of them was the saving of the nations. "We turn to the Gentiles," said the apostle; and that was a blessed turning for you and for me. Was it not? They that were bidden to the feast were not worthy, and the master of the house, being angry, invited other guests. Mark, "being angry"! What did he do when he was angry? Why, he did the most gracious thing of all; he said, "Go ye out into the highways and hedges, and as many as ye shall find bid to the supper." Sin abounded, for Israel would not enter the feast of love; but grace did much more abound, for the heathen entered the kingdom.

31

*The heathen world at that time* was sunk in the blackest darkness, and sin abounded. You have only to study ancient history and you will fetch a heavy sigh to think that men could be so vile. A poor and unlettered people were chosen of God to receive the gospel of Jesus, and they went about telling of an atoning Savior, in their own simple way, until the Roman empire was entirely changed. Light and peace and truth came into the world, and drove away slavery and tyranny and bestial lust. Where sin abounded, grace did much more abound. What wonderful characters were produced in the terrible reign of Diocletian! What consecration to God was seen in the confessors! What fearlessness in common Christians! What invincible loyalty to Christ in the martyrs! Out of barbarians the Lord made saints, and the degraded rose to holiness sublime.

If I were to ask you, now, to give the best illustrations of grace abounding in individuals, I think your impulse would be to choose *men in whom sin once abounded.* What characters do we preach of most, when we would magnify the grace of God? We talk of David, and Manasseh, and swearing Peter, and the dying thief, and Saul of Tarsus, and the woman that was a sinner. If we want to show where grace abounded, we naturally turn our eyes to the place where sin abounded. Is it not so? Therefore, I need not give you any more cases—it is proven that where sin abounded, grace did much more abound.

## Grace over Sin in Our Lives

Lastly; and this is what I want to hold you to, dear friends, at this time: THIS HOLDS TRUE TO EACH ONE OF US.

Let me take the case of the *open sinner.* What have you been? Have you grossly sinned? Have you defiled your body with unhallowed passions? Have you been dishonest to your fellow-men? Does some scarlet sin stain your conscience, even as you sit in the pew? Have you grown hardened in sin by long perseverance in it? Are you conscious that you have frequently, wilfully, and resolutely sinned? Are you getting old, and have you been soaking these seventy years in the crimson dye of sin till you are saturated through and through with its color? Have you even been an implacable opponent of the gospel? Have you persecuted the saints of God? Have you tried by argument to batter down the gospel, or by ridicule to put it to reproach?

Then hear this text: "Where sin abounded, grace did much more abound"; and as it was in the beginning, it is now and ever shall be, till this world shall end. The grace of God, if thou believest in the Lord Jesus Christ, will triumph over the greatness of thy wickedness. "All manner of sin and blasphemy shall be forgiven unto men." Throw down your weapons of rebellion; surrender at discretion; kiss the pierced hand of Jesus which is now held out to you, and this very moment you shall be forgiven, and you shall go your way a pardoned man, to begin a new life, and to bear witness that "where sin abounded, grace did much more abound."

Perhaps this does not touch you, my friend. Listen to my next word which is addressed to *the instructed sinner*. You are a person whose religious education has made you aware of the guilt of sin; you have read your Bible, and you have heard truthful preaching; and although you have never been a gross open sinner, yet you know that your life teems with sins of omission and commission. You know that you have sinned against light and knowledge. You have done despite to a tender conscience very often; and therefore you rightly judge that

33

you are even a greater sinner than the more openly profane.

Be it so; I take you at that. Do not run back from it. Let it be so; for "where sin abounded, grace did much more abound." Oh, that you may be as much instructed in the remedy, as you are instructed in the disease! Oh, that you may have as clear a view of the righteousness of Christ, as you have of your own unrighteousness! Christ's work is a divine work, broad enough to cover all your iniquity, and to conquer all your sin. Believe this! Give glory to God by believing it; and according to your faith, so be it unto you.

I address another, who does not answer either of these two descriptions exactly; but he has lately begun to seek mercy, and the more he prays the more he is *tempted*. Horrible suggestions rush into his mind; damnable thoughts beset and bewilder him. Ah, my friend, I know what this means: the nearer you are to mercy, the nearer you seem to get to hell-gate! When you most solemnly mean to do good, you feel another law in your members bringing you into captivity. You grow worse where you hoped you would have grown better.

Very well, then; grip my text firmly as for your life: "Where sin abounded, grace did much more abound." If a whole legion of devils should be let loose upon you, Christ will glorify himself by mastering them all. If now you cannot repent, nor pray, nor do anything, remember that text, "When we were yet without strength, in due time Christ died for the ungodly." Look over the heads of all these doubts, and devils, and inabilities, and see Jesus lifted on the cross, like the brazen serpent upon the pole; and look thou to him, and the fiery serpents shall flee away from thee, and thou shalt live. Believe this text to be true, for true it is: "Where sin abounded, grace did much more abound."

"Ah!" saith another, "my case is still worse, sir; I am of a *despondent* turn of mind; I always look upon the black side of everything, and now if I read a promise I am sure it is not for me. If I see a threatening in God's Word, I am sure it is for me. I have no hope. I do not seem as if I should ever have any. I am in a dungeon into which no light can enter: it is dark, dark, dark, and worse darkness is coming. While you are trying to comfort me, I put the comfort away." I know you. You are like the poor creature in the Psalm, of whom we read—"His soul abhorreth all manner of meat." Even the gospel itself he cannot relish. Yes; I know you; you are writing bitter things against yourself: this morning you have been newly dipping your pen in gall; but your writing is that of a poor bewildered creature; it is not to be taken notice of. I see your writing, in text hand, great black words of condemnation; but there is nothing in them all.

Verily, verily I say unto thee, thine handwriting shall be blotted out, and the curse, causeless, shall not come. Thus saith the Lord, "Your covenant with death shall be disannulled, and your agreement with hell shall not stand, for the Lord Jesus Christ has redeemed you, and where sin abounded, grace shall much more abound." Broken in pieces, all asunder, ground between the millstones, reduced to nothing, yet believe this revelation of God, that where sin abounded, grace did much more abound." Notice that *"much more"*—"much more abound." If thou canst grip it, and know it to be of a certainty the great principle upon which God acts, that grace shall outstrip sin, then there is hope of thee; nay, more than hope, there is salvation for thee on the spot. If thou believest in Jesus, whom God has set forth to be a propitiation for sin, thou art forgiven.

Oh, my hearers, do not despise this grace! Come, and partake of it. Does any one say, as Paul foresaw that some would say, "Let us sin, that grace may abound"? Ah, then, such an infamous inference is the mark of the reprobate, and your damnation is just. He that turns God's mercy into a reason for sin, has within him something worse than a heart of stone: surely his conscience is seared with a hot iron. Beloved, I hope better things of you, for I trust that on the contrary, the sound of the silver bells of infinite love, free pardon, abounding grace, will make you hasten to the hospital of mercy, that you may receive healing for your sinfulness, strength for your feebleness, and joy for your sorrow. Lord, grant that in this house, in every case wherein sin has abounded, grace may yet more abound, for Jesus' sake! Amen.

Early in Spurgeon's ministry, before the Metropolitan Tabernacle had been built, he preached at the Surrey Gardens Music Hall in order to accommodate his large audiences. His first sermon there, which he delivered on October 19, 1856, quickly became a debacle. Denied the use of Exeter Hall, his attempt to preach in an indoor place with a total seating capacity of ten thousand seemed impossible to many. At first, everything proceeded normally, but just after he began to pray someone perversely shouted "Fire!" and within minutes a panic had erupted that left seven people dead and twenty-eight others injured. Spurgeon was blamed by many for the catastrophe, and his burden was made even greater by the fact that only a month earlier his wife had given birth to twins. Only twenty-two at the time, this incident was to haunt him for the rest of his life.

"Compel Them to Come In," delivered on December 5, 1858, at the Surrey Gardens Music Hall, is representative of Spurgeon's evangelistic sermons that were aimed directly at sinners. Some consider it his "sermon with the greatest soul-saving testimony," and of it Spurgeon himself wrote "The sermon entitled 'Compel them to come in' has been so signally owned of God, that scarcely a week occurs without some case of its usefulness coming to light."

CHAPTER TWO

# *Compel Them to Come In*

*Compel them to come in (Luke 14:23).*

I feel in such a haste to go out and obey this commandment this morning, by compelling those to come in who are now tarrying in the highways and hedges, that I cannot wait for an introduction, but must at once set about my business.

Hear then, O ye that are strangers to the truth as it is in Jesus—hear then the message that I have to bring you. Ye have fallen, fallen in your father Adam; ye have fallen also in yourselves, by your daily sin and your constant iniquity; you have provoked the anger of the Most High; and as assuredly as you have sinned, so certainly must God punish you if you persevere in your iniquity, for the Lord is a God of justice, and will by no means spare the guilty. But have you not heard, hath it not long been spoken in your ears, that God, in his infinite mercy, has devised a way whereby, without any infringement upon his honor, he can have mercy upon you, the guilty and the undeserving?

To you I speak; and my voice is unto you, O sons of men; Jesus Christ, very God of very God, hath descended from heaven, and was made in the likeness of sinful flesh. Begotten of the Holy Ghost, he was born of the Virgin Mary; he lived in this world a life of exemplary holiness, and of the deepest suffering, till at last he gave himself up to die for our sins, "the just for the unjust, to bring us to God." And now the plan of salvation is simply declared unto you—"Whosoever believeth in the Lord Jesus Christ shall be saved." For you who have violated all the precepts of God, and have disdained his mercy and dared his vengeance, there is yet mercy proclaimed, for "whosoever calleth upon the name of the Lord shall be saved." "For this is a faithful saying and worthy of all acceptation, that Christ Jesus came into the world to save sinners, of whom I am chief;" "whosoever cometh unto him he will in no wise cast out, for he is able also to save unto the uttermost them that come unto God by him, seeing he ever liveth to make intercession for us."

Now all that God asks of you—and this he gives you—is that you will simply look at his bleeding dying son, and trust your souls in the hands of him whose name alone can save from death and hell. Is it not a marvellous thing, that the proclamation of this gospel does not receive the unanimous consent of men? One would think that as soon as ever this was preached, "That whosoever believeth shall have eternal life,"every one of you, "casting away every man his sins and his iniquities," would lay hold on Jesus Christ, and look alone to his cross. But alas! such is the desperate evil of our nature, such the pernicious depravity of our character, that this message is despised, the invitation to the gospel feast is rejected, and there are many of you who are this day enemies of

God by wicked works, enemies to the God who preaches Christ to you to-day, enemies to him who sent his Son to give his life a ransom for many. Strange I say it is that it should be so, yet nevertheless it is the fact, and hence the necessity for the command of the text,—"Compel them to come in."

Children of God, ye who have believed, I shall have little or nothing to say to you this morning; I am going straight to my business—I am going after those that will not come—those that are in the byeways and hedges, and God going with me, it is my duty now to fulfill this command, "Compel them to come in."

First, I must *find you out;* secondly, I will go to work to *compel you to come in.*

## I Must Find You Out

If you read the verses that precede the text, you will find an amplification of this command: "Go out quickly into the streets and lanes of the city, and bring in hither the poor, the maimed, the halt, and the blind;" and then, afterwards, "Go out into the highways," bring in the vagrants, the highwaymen, "and into the hedges," bring in those that have no resting-place for their heads, and are lying under the hedges to rest, bring them in also, and "compel them to come in." Yes, I see you this morning, you that are *poor.* I am to compel *you* to come in. You are poor in circumstances, but this is no barrier to the kingdom of heaven, for God hath not exempted from his grace the man that shivers in rags, and who is destitute of bread. In fact, if there be any distinction made, the distinction is on your side, and for your benefit—"Unto you is the word of salvation sent;" "For the poor have the gospel preached unto them."

But especially I must speak to you who are *poor, spiritually.* You have no faith, you have no virtue, you have no good work, you have no grace, and what is poverty worse still, you have no hope. Ah, my Master has sent *you* a gracious invitation. Come and welcome to the marriage feast of his love. "Whosoever will, let him come and take of the waters of life freely." Come, I must lay hold upon you, though you be defiled with foulest filth, and though you have nought but rags upon your back, though your own righteousness has become as filthy clouts, yet must I lay hold upon you, and invite you first, and even compel you to come in.

And now I see you again. You are not only poor, but you are *maimed.* There was a time when you thought you could work out your own salvation without God's help, when you could perform good works, attend to ceremonies, and get to heaven by yourselves; but now you are maimed, the sword of the law has cut off your hands, and now you can work no longer; you say, with bitter sorrow—

> The best performance of my hands,
> Dares not appear before thy throne.

You have lost all power now to obey the law; you feel that when you would do good, evil is present with you. You are maimed; you have given up, as a forlorn hope, all attempt to save yourself, because you are maimed and your arms are gone. But you are worse off than that, for if you could not work your way to heaven, yet you could walk your way there along the road by faith; but you are maimed in the feet as well as in the hands; you feel that you cannot believe, that you cannot repent, that you cannot obey the stipulations of the gospel. You feel that you

are utterly undone, powerless in every respect to do anything that can be pleasing to God. In fact, you are crying
out—

> Oh, could I but believe,
>   Then all would easy be,
> I would, but cannot, Lord relieve,
>   My help must come from thee.

To you am I sent also. Before *you* am I to lift up the blood-
stained banner of the cross, to you am I to preach this
gospel, "Whoso calleth upon the name of the Lord shall
be saved;" and unto you am I to cry "Whosoever will, let
him come and take of the water of life freely."

There is yet another class. You are *halt*. You are halting
between two opinions. You are sometimes seriously inclined, and at another time worldly gaiety calls you
away. What little progress you do make in religion is but
a limp. You have a little strength, but that is so little that
you make but painful progress. Ah, limping brother, to
you also is the word of this salvation sent. Though you
halt between two opinions, the master sends me to you
with this message: "How long halt ye between two opinions? if God be God, serve him; if Baal be God, serve
him." Consider thy ways; set thine house in order, for
thou shalt die and not live. Because I will do this, prepare to meet thy God, O Israel! Halt no longer, but decide
for God and his truth.

And yet I see another class,—*the blind*. Yes, you that
cannot see yourselves, that think yourselves good when
you are full of evil, that put bitter for sweet and sweet for
bitter, darkness for light and light for darkness; to you
am I sent. You, blind souls that cannot see your lost estate, that do not believe that sin is so exceedingly sinful

as it is, and who will not be persuaded to think that God is a just and righteous God, to you am I sent. To you too that cannot see the Savior, that see no beauty in him that you should desire him; who see no excellence in virtue, no glories in religion, no happiness in serving God, no delight in being his children; to you, also, am I sent.

Ay, to whom am I not sent if I take my text? For it goes further than this—it not only gives a particular description, so that each individual case may be met, but afterwards it makes a general sweep, and says, "Go into the highways and hedges." Here we bring in all ranks and conditions of men—my lord upon his horse in the highway, and the woman trudging about her business, the thief waylaying the traveller—all these are in the highway, and they are all to be compelled to come in, and there away in the hedges there lie some poor souls whose refuges of lies are swept away, and who are seeking now to find some little shelter for their weary heads, to you, also, are we sent this morning. This is the universal command—compel them to come in.

Now, I pause after having described the character, I pause to look at the herculean labor that lies before me. Well did Melanchthon say, "Old Adam was too strong for young Melanchthon." As well might a little child seek to compel a Samson, as I seek to lead a sinner to the cross of Christ. And yet my Master sends me about the errand. Lo, I see the great mountain before me of human depravity and stolid indifference, but by faith I cry, "Who art thou, O great mountain? before Zerubbabel thou shalt become a plain." Does my Master say, compel them to come in? Then, though the sinner be like Samson and I a child, I shall lead him with a thread. If God saith *do* it, if I attempt it in faith *it shall be done;* and if with a groaning, struggling, and weeping heart, I so seek this day to compel sinners to come to Christ, the sweet compulsions of the Holy Spirit shall go with every word, and some indeed shall be compelled to come in.

## I Compel You to Come In

And now to the work—directly to the work. Unconverted, unreconciled, unregenerate men and women, I am to COMPEL YOU TO COME IN. Permit me first of all to accost you in the highways of sin and tell you over again my errand. The King of heaven this morning sends a gracious invitation to you. He says, "As I live, saith the Lord, I have no pleasure in the death of him that dieth, but had rather that he should turn unto me and live." "Come now and let us reason together saith the Lord, though your sins be as scarlet they shall be as wool; though they be red like crimson they shall be whiter than snow." Dear brother, it makes my heart rejoice to think that I should have such good news to tell you, and yet I confess my soul is heavy because I see you do not think it good news, but turn away from it, and do not give it due regard. Permit me to tell you what the King has done for you. He knew your guilt, he foresaw that you would ruin yourself. He knew that his justice would demand your blood, and in order that this difficulty might be escaped, that his justice might have its full due, and that you might yet be saved, *Jesus Christ hath died*.

Will you just for a moment glance at this picture. You see that man there on his knees in the garden of Gethsemane, sweating drops of blood. You see this next; you see that miserable sufferer tied to a pillar and lashed with terrible scourges, till the shoulder bones are seen like white islands in the midst of a sea of blood. Again you see this third picture; it is the same man hanging on the cross with hands extended, and with feet nailed fast, dying, groaning, bleeding; methought the picture spoke and said, "It is finished." Now all this hath Jesus Christ of Nazareth done, in order that God might consistently with his justice pardon sin; and the message to you this morning is this—"Believe on the Lord Jesus Christ and thou shalt be saved." That is trust him, renounce thy works, and thy ways, and set thine heart alone on this man, who gave himself for sinners.

Well brother, I have told you the message, what sayest thou unto it? Do you turn away? You tell me it is nothing to you; you cannot listen to it; that you will hear me by-and-by; but you will go your ways this day and attend to your farm and merchandise. Stop brother, I was not told merely to tell you and then go about my business. No; I am told to compel you to come in; and permit me to observe to you before I further go, that there is one thing I can say—and to which God is my witness this morning, that I am in earnest with you in my desire that you should comply with this command of God. You may despise your own salvation, but I do not despise it; you may go away and forget what you shall hear, but you will please to remember that the things I now say cost me many a groan ere I came here to utter them. My inmost soul is speaking out to you, my poor brother, when I beseech you by him that liveth and was dead, and is alive for evermore, consider my master's message which he bids me now address to you.

## I Command You to Come In

But do you spurn it? Do you still refuse it? Then I must change my tone a minute. I will not merely tell you the message, and invite you as I do with all earnestness, and sincere affection—I will go further. Sinner, in God's name I *command* you to repent and believe. Do you ask me whence my authority? I am an ambassador of heaven. My credentials, some of them secret, and in my own heart; and others of them open before you this day in the seals of my ministry, sitting and standing in this hall, where God has given me many souls for my hire. As God the everlasting one hath given me a commission to preach his gospel, I command you to believe in the Lord Jesus Christ; not on my own authority, but on the authority of him who said, "Go ye into all the world and preach the gospel to every creature;" and then annexed this solemn sanction, "He that believeth and is baptized shall be saved, but he that believeth not shall be damned."

Reject my message, and remember, "He that despised Moses's law, died without mercy under two or three witnesses: of how much sorer punishment, suppose ye, shall he be thought worthy, who hath trodden under foot the Son of God." An ambassador is not to stand below the man with whom he deals, for we stand higher. If the minister chooses to take his proper rank, girded with the omnipotence of God, and anointed with his holy unction, he is to command men, and speak with all authority compelling them to come in: "command, exhort, rebuke with all longsuffering."

## I Exhort You to Flee to Christ

But do you turn away and say you will not be commanded? Then again will I change my note. If that avails not, all other means shall be tried. My brother, I come to you simple of speech, and I *exhort* you to flee to Christ. O my brother, dost thou know what a loving Christ he is? Let me tell thee from my own soul what I know of him. I, too once despised him. He knocked at the door of my heart and I refused to open it. He came to me, times without number, morning by morning, and night by night; he checked me in my conscience and spoke to me by his Spirit, and when, at last, the thunders of the law prevailed in my conscience, I thought that Christ was cruel and unkind. O I can never forgive myself that I should have thought so ill of him.

But what a loving reception did I have when I went to him. I thought he would smite me, but his hand was not clenched in anger but opened wide in mercy. I thought full sure that his eyes would dart lightning-flashes of wrath upon me; but, instead thereof, they were full of tears. He fell upon my neck and kissed me; he took off my rags and did clothe me with his righteousness, and caused my soul to sing aloud for joy; while in the house of my heart and in the house of his church there was music and dancing, because his son that he had lost was found, and he that was dead was made alive.

I exhort you, then, to look to Jesus Christ and to be lightened. Sinner, you will never regret,—I will be bondsman for my Master that you will never regret it,—you will have no sigh to go back to your state of condemnation; you shall go out of Egypt and shall go into the promised land and shall find it flowing with milk and honey. The trials of Christian life you shall find heavy, but you will find grace will make them light. And as for the joys and delights of being a child of God, if I lie this day you shall charge me with it in days to come. If you will taste and see that the Lord is good, I am not afraid but that you shall find that he is not only good, but better than human lips ever can describe.

## I Appeal to Your Own Self-Interests

I know not what arguments to use with you. I appeal to your own self-interests. Oh my poor friend, would it not be better for you to be reconciled to the God of heaven, than to be his enemy? What are you getting by opposing God? Are you the happier for being his enemy? Answer, pleasure-seeker: hast thou found delights in that cup? Answer me, self-righteous man: hast thou found rest for the sole of thy foot in all thy works? Oh thou that goest about to establish thine own righteousness, I charge thee let conscience speak. Hast thou found it to be a happy path? Ah, my friend, "Wherefore dost thou spend thy money for that which is not bread, and thy labor for that which satisfieth not; hearken diligently unto me, and eat ye that which is good, and let your soul delight itself in fatness." I exhort you by everything that is sacred and solemn, everything that is important and eternal, flee for your lives, look not behind you, stay not in all the plain, stay not until you have proved, and found an interest in the blood of Jesus Christ, that blood which cleanseth us from all sin.

Are you still cold and indifferent? Will not the blind man permit me to lead him to the feast? Will not my maimed brother put his hand upon my shoulder and permit me to assist him to the banquet? Will not the poor man allow me to walk side-by-side with him? Must I use some stronger words. Must I use some other compulsion to compel you to come in? Sinners, this one thing I am resolved upon this morning, if you be not saved ye shall be without excuse. Ye, from the grey-headed down to the tender age of childhood, if ye this day lay not hold on Christ, your blood shall be on your own head. If there be power in man to bring his fellow, (as there is when man is helped by the Holy Spirit) that power shall be exercised this morning, God helping me.

Come, I am not to be put off by your rebuffs: if my exhortation fails, I must come to something else. My brother I ENTREAT you, I entreat you stop and consider. Do you know what it is you are rejecting this morning? You are rejecting Christ, your only Savior. "Other foundation can no man lay;" "there is none other name given among men whereby we must be saved." My brother, I cannot bear that ye should do this, for I remember what you are forgetting: the day is coming when you will want a Savior. It is not long ere weary months shall have ended, and your strength begin to decline; your pulse shall fail you, your strength shall depart, and you and the grim monster—death, must face each other. What will you do in the swellings of Jordan without a Savior? Death-beds are stony things without the Lord Jesus Christ. It is an awful thing to die anyhow; he that hath the best hope, and the most triumphant faith, finds that death is not a thing to laugh at. It is a terrible thing to pass from the seen to the unseen, from the mortal to the immortal, from time to eternity, and you will find it hard to go through the iron gates of death without the sweet wings of angels to conduct you to the portals of the skies. It will be a hard thing to die without Christ.

I cannot help thinking of you. I see you acting the suicide this morning, and I picture myself standing at your bedside and hearing your cries, and knowing that you are dying without hope. I cannot bear that. I think I am standing by your coffin now, and looking into your clay-

cold face, and saying, "This man despised Christ and neglected the great salvation." I think what bitter tears I
shall weep then, if I think that I have been unfaithful to
you, and how those eyes fast closed in death, shall seem
to chide me and say, "Minister, I attended the music hall,
but you were not in earnest with me; you amused me,
you preached to me, but you did not plead with me. You
did not know what Paul meant when he said, 'As though
God did beseech you by us we pray you in Christ's stead,
be ye reconciled to God.'"

## I Entreat You Because I Must

I entreat you let this message enter your heart for another reason. I picture myself standing at the bar of God.
As the Lord liveth, the day of judgment is coming. You
believe that? You are not an infidel; your conscience
would not permit you to doubt the Scripture. Perhaps
you may have pretended to do so, but you cannot. You
feel there must be a day when God shall judge the world
in righteousness. I see you standing in the midst of that
throng, and the eye of God is fixed on you. It seems to you
that he is not looking anywhere else, but only upon you,
and he summons you before him; and he reads your sins,
and he cries, "Depart ye cursed into everlasting fire in
hell!"

My hearer, I cannot bear to think of you in that position; it seems as if every hair on my head must stand on
end to think of any hearer of mine being damned. Will
you picture yourselves in that position? The word has
gone forth, "Depart, ye cursed." Do you see the pit as it
opens to swallow you up? Do you listen to the shrieks
and the yells of those who have preceded you to that eternal lake of torment? Instead of picturing the scene, I

turn to you with the words of the inspired prophet, and I say, "Who among us shall dwell with the devouring fire? Who among us shall dwell with everlasting burnings?" Oh! my brother, I cannot let you put away religion thus; no, I think of what is to come after death. I should be destitute of all humanity if I should see a person about to poison himself, and did not dash away the cup; or if I saw another about to plunge from London Bridge, if I did not assist in preventing him from doing so; and I should be worse than a fiend if I did not now, with all love, and kindness, and earnestness, beseech you to "lay hold on eternal life," "to labour not for the meat that perisheth, but for the meat that endureth unto everlasting life."

Some hyper-Calvinist would tell me I am wrong in so doing. I cannot help it. I must do it. As I must stand before my Judge at last, I feel that I shall not make full proof of my ministry unless I entreat with many tears that ye would be saved, that ye would look unto Jesus Christ and receive his glorious salvation.

But does not this avail? are all our entreaties lost upon you; do you turn a deaf ear? Then again I change my note. Sinner, I have pleaded with you as a man pleadeth with his friend, and were it for my *own* life I could not speak more earnestly this morning than I do speak concerning *yours*. I did feel earnest about my own soul, but not a whit more than I do about the souls of my congregation this morning; and therefore, if ye put away these entreaties I have something else;—I must *threaten* you. You shall not always have such warnings as these. A day is coming, when hushed shall be the voice of every gospel minister, at least for you; for your ear shall be cold in death. It shall not be any more threatening; it shall be the fulfilment of the threatening. There shall be no promise, no proclamations of pardon and of mercy; no peace-speaking blood, but you shall be in the land where the Sabbath is all swallowed up in everlasting nights of misery, and where the preachings of the gospel are forbidden because they would be unavailing. I charge you then, listen to this voice that now addresses your conscience; for if not, God shall speak to you in his wrath, and say unto you in his hot displeasure, "I called and ye refused; I stretched out my hand and no man regarded; therefore will I mock at your calamity; I will laugh when your fear cometh."

Sinner, I threaten you again. Remember, it is but a short time you may have to hear these warnings. You imagine that your life will be long, but do you know how short it is? Have you ever tried to think how frail you are? Did you ever see a body when it has been cut in pieces by the anatomist? Did you ever see such a marvellous thing as the human frame?

> Strange, a harp of a thousand strings,
> Should keep in tune so long.

Let but one of those cords be twisted, let but a mouthful of food go in the wrong direction, and you may die. The slightest chance, as we have it, may send you swift to death, when God wills it. Strong men have been killed by the smallest and slightest accident, and so may you. In the chapel, in the house of God, men have dropped down dead. How often do we hear of men falling in our streets—rolling out of time into eternity, by some sudden stroke. And are you sure that heart of yours is quite sound? Is the blood circulating with all accuracy? Are you quite sure of that? And if it be so, how long shall it be?

53

O, perhaps there are some of you here that shall never see Christmas-day; it may be the mandate has gone forth already, "Set thine house in order, for thou shalt die and not live." Out of this vast congregation, I might with accuracy tell how many will be dead in a year; but certain it is that the whole of us shall never meet together again in any one assembly. Some out of this vast crowd, perhaps some two or three, shall depart ere the new year shall be ushered in. I remind you, then, my brother, that either the gate of salvation may be shut, or else you may be out of the place where the gate of mercy stands. Come, then, let the threatening have power with you. I do not threaten because I would alarm without cause, but in hopes that a brother's threatening may drive you to the place where God hath prepared the feast of the gospel.

## What Is It that Keeps You from Christ?

And now, *must I turn hopelessly away?* Have I exhausted all that I can say? No, I will come to you again. Tell me what it is, my brother, that keeps you from Christ. I hear one say, "Oh, sir, it is because I feel myself too guilty." That cannot be, my friend, that cannot be. "But, sir, I am the chief of sinners." Friend, you are not. The chief of sinners died and went to heaven many years ago; his name was Saul of Tarsus, afterwards called Paul the apostle. He was the chief of sinners, I know he spoke the truth. "No," but you say still, "I am too vile." You cannot be viler than the *chief* of sinners. You must, at least, be second worst. Even supposing you are the worst now alive, you are second worst, for he was chief.

But suppose you are the worst, is not that the very reason why you should come to Christ. The worse a man is, the more reason he should go to the hospital or physician. The more poor you are, the more reason you should accept the charity of another. Now, Christ does not want any merits of yours. He gives freely. The worse you are, the more welcome you are. But let me ask you a question: Do you think you will ever get better by stopping away from Christ? If so, you know very little as yet of the way of salvation at all. No, sir, the longer you stay the worse you will grow; your hope will grow weaker, your despair will become stronger; the nail with which Satan has fastened you down will be more firmly clenched, and you will be less hopeful than ever. Come, I beseech you, recollect there is nothing to be gained by delay, but by delay everything may be lost.

"But," cries another, "I feel I cannot believe." No, my friend, and you never will believe if you look first at your believing. Remember, I am not come to invite you to faith, but am come to invite you to Christ. But you say, "What is the difference?" Why, just this. If you first of all say, "I want to believe a thing," you never do it. But your first inquiry must be, "What is this thing that I am to believe?" Then will faith come as the consequence of that search. Our first business has not to do with faith, but with Christ.

Come, I beseech you, on Calvary's mount, and see the cross. Behold the Son of God, he who made the heavens and the earth, dying for your sins. Look to him, is there not power in him to save? Look at his face so full of pity. Is there not love in his heart to prove him *willing* to save? Sure sinner, the sight of Christ will help thee to believe. Do not believe first, and then go to Christ, or else thy faith will be a worthless thing; go to Christ without any faith, and cast thyself upon him, sink or swim.

But I hear another cry, "Oh sir, you do not know how

often I have been invited, how long I have rejected the Lord." I do not know, and I do not want to know; all I know is that my Master has sent me, to compel you to come in; so come along with you now. You may have rejected a thousand invitations; don't make this the thousandth-and-one. You have been up to the house of God, and you have only been gospel hardened. But do I not see a tear in your eye? Come my brother don't be hardened by this morning's sermon. O, Spirit of the living God come and melt this heart for it has never been melted, and compel him to come in! I cannot let you go on such idle excuses as that; if you have lived so many years slighting Christ, there are so many reasons why now you should not slight him.

But did I hear you whisper that this was not a convenient time? Then what must I say to you? When will that convenient time come? Shall it come when you are in hell? Will that time be convenient? Shall it come when you are on your dying bed, and the death throttle is in your throat—shall it come then? Or when the burning sweat is scalding your brow; and then again, when the cold clammy sweat is there, shall those be convenient times? When pains are racking you, and you are on the borders of the tomb?

No, sir, this morning is the convenient time. May God make it so. Remember, I have no authority to ask you to come to Christ *to-morrow*. The Master has given you no invitation to come to him next Tuesday. The invitation is, "*To-day* if ye will hear his voice, harden not your hearts as in the provocation," for the Spirit saith "to-day." "Come *now* and let us reason together;" why should you put it off? It may be the last warning you shall ever have. Put it off, and you may never weep again in chapel. You may never have so earnest a discourse addressed to you.

You may not be pleaded with as I would plead with you now. You may go away, and God may say, "He is given unto idols, let him alone." He shall throw the reins upon your neck; and then, mark—your course is sure, but it is sure damnation and swift destruction.

## I Pray and Weep for You

And now again, is it all in vain? Will you not now come to Christ? Then what more can I do? I have but one more resort, and that shall be tried. I can be permitted to weep for you; I can be allowed to pray for you. You shall scorn the address if you like; you shall laugh at the preacher; you shall call him fanatic if you will; he will not chide you, he will bring no accusation against you to the great Judge. Your offense, so far as he is concerned, is forgiven before it is committed; but you will remember that the message that you are rejecting this morning is a message from one who loves you, and it is given to you also by the lips of one who loves you. You will recollect that you may play your soul away with the devil, that you may listlessly think it a matter of no importance; but there lives at least one who is in earnest about your soul, and one who before he came here wrestled with his God for strength to preach to you, and who when he has gone from this place will not forget his hearers of this morning.

I say again, when words fail us we can give tears—for words and tears are the arms with which gospel ministers compel men to come in. You do not know, and I suppose could not believe, how anxious a man whom God has called to the ministry feels about his congregation, and especially about some of them. I heard but the other day of a young man who attended here a long time, and his father's hope was that he would be brought to Christ. He became acquainted, however, with an infidel; and now he neglects his business, and lives in a daily course of sin. I saw his father's poor wan face; I did not ask him to tell me the story himself, for I felt it was raking up a trouble and opening a sore; I fear, sometimes, that good man's grey hairs may be brought with sorrow to the grave.

Young men, you do not pray for yourselves, but your mothers wrestle for you. You will not think of your own souls, but your father's anxiety is exercised for you. I have been at prayer meetings, when I have heard children of God pray there, and they could not have prayed with more earnestness and more intensity of anguish if they had been each of them seeking their own soul's salvation. And is it not strange that we should be ready to move heaven and earth for your salvation, and that still you should have no thought for *yourselves*, no regard to eternal things?

Now I turn for one moment to some here. There are some of you here members of Christian churches, who make a profession of religion, but unless I be mistaken in you—and I shall be happy if I am—your profession is a lie. You do not live up to it, you dishonor it; you can live in the perpetual practice of absenting yourselves from God's house, if not in sins worse than that. Now I ask such of you who do not adorn the doctrine of God your Savior, do you imagine that you can call me your pastor, and yet that my soul cannot tremble over you and in secret weep for you? Again, I say it may be but little concern to you how you defile the garments of your Christianity, but it is a great concern to God's hidden ones, who sigh and cry, and groan for the iniquities of the professors of Zion.

Now does anything else remain to the minister besides weeping and prayer? Yes, there is one thing else. God has given to his servants not the power of regeneration, but he has given them something akin to it. It is impossible for any man to regenerate his neighbor; and yet how are men born to God? Does not the apostle say of such an one that he was begotten by him in his bonds? Now the minister has a power given him of God, to be considered both the father and the mother of those born to God, for the apostle said he travailed in birth for souls till Christ was formed in them.

What can we do then? We can now appeal to the Spirit. I know I have preached the gospel, that I have preached it earnestly. I challenge my Master to honor his own promise. He has said it shall not return unto me void, and it shall not. It is in his hands, not mine. I cannot compel you, but thou O Spirit of God who hast the key of the heart, thou canst compel. Did you ever notice in that chapter of the Revelation, where it says, "Behold I stand at the door and knock," a few verses before, the same person is described, as he who hath the key of David. So that if knocking will not avail, he has the key and can and will come in. Now if the knocking of an earnest minister prevail not with you this morning, there remains still that secret opening of the heart by the Spirit, so that you shall be compelled.

I thought it my duty to labor with you as though *I* must do it; now I throw it into my Master's hands. It cannot be his will that we should travail in birth, and yet not bring forth spiritual children. It is with *him;* he is master of the heart, and the day shall declare it, that some of you constrained by sovereign grace have become the willing captives of the all-conquering Jesus, and have bowed your hearts to him through the sermon of this morning.

*A great advocate of open-air preaching, Spurgeon deliv-
ered "Heaven and Hell" on September 4, 1855, in a field
beside King Edward's Road in Hackney. He had not originally intended it for publication and apologized for any
faults it might have in composition, noting that this sermon "was watered by many prayers of the faithful in
Zion." In "Heaven and Hell" Spurgeon contrasts the glory
of heaven with the terrors of hell to reach a diverse audience composed of the saved and the unsaved and people of
all different ages. "Heaven and Hell" is uniquely intrigu-
ing because it concludes with a description of Spurgeon's
famous conversion six years earlier.*

# CHAPTER THREE

## *Heaven and Hell*

*And I say unto you, That many shall come from the east and west, and shall sit down with Abraham, and Isaac, and Jacob, in the kingdom of heaven. But the children of the kingdom shall be cast out into outer darkness: there shall be weeping and gnashing of teeth (Matt. 8:11, 12).*

This is a land where plain speaking is allowed, and where the people are willing to afford a fair hearing to any one who can tell them that which is worth their attention. To-night I am quite certain of an attentive audience, for I know you too well to suppose otherwise. This field, as you are all aware, is private property. And I would just give a suggestion to those who go out in the open air to preach—that it is far better to get into a field or a plot of unoccupied building ground, than to block up the roads and stop business; it is moreover far better to be somewhere under protection, so that we can at once prevent disturbance.

To-night, I shall, I hope, encourage you to seek the road to heaven. I shall also have to utter some very sharp things concerning the end of the lost in the pit of hell. Upon both these subjects I will try and speak, as God helps me. But I beseech you, as you love your souls, weigh right and wrong this night; see whether what I say be the truth of God. If it be not, reject it utterly, and cast it away; but if it is, at your peril disregard it; for as you shall answer before God, the great Judge of heaven and earth, it will go ill with you if the words of his servant and of his Scripture be despised.

My text has two parts. The first is very agreeable to my mind, and gives me pleasure; the second is terrible in the extreme; but since they are both the truth, they must be preached. The first part of my text is, "I say unto you, that many shall come from the east and west, and shall sit down with Abraham, and Isaac, and Jacob, in the kingdom of heaven." The sentence which I call the black, dark, and threatening part is this: "But the children of the kingdom shall be cast out into outer darkness: there shall be weeping and gnashing of teeth."

## The Promise

Let us take the first part. Here is a MOST GLORIOUS PROMISE. I will read it again—"Many shall come from the east and west, and shall sit down with Abraham, and Isaac, and Jacob, in the kingdom of heaven." I like that text, because it tells me what heaven is, and gives me a beautiful picture of it. It says, it is a place where I shall sit down with Abraham, and Isaac, and Jacob. O what a sweet thought that is for the working-man. He often wipes the hot sweat from his face, and he wonders whether there is a land where he shall have to toil no longer. He scarcely ever eats a mouthful of bread that is not moistened with the sweat of his brow. Often he comes home weary, and flings himself upon his couch, perhaps too tired to sleep. He says, "Oh! is there no land where I can rest? Is there no place where I can sit, and for once let these weary limbs be still? Is there no land where I can be quiet?" Yes, thou son of toil and labor,

> There is a happy land
> Far, far, away,—

where toil and labor are unknown. Beyond yon blue welkin there a city fair and bright, its walls are jasper, and its light is brighter than the sun. There "the weary are at rest, and the wicked cease from troubling." Immortal spirits are yonder, who never wipe sweat from their brow, for "they sow not, neither do they reap;" they have not to toil and labor.

> There on a green and flow'ry mount
> Their wearied souls shall sit:
> And with transporting joys recount
> The labors of their feet.

To my mind, one of the best views of heaven is that *it is a land of rest*—especially to the working-man. Those who have not to work hard, think they will love heaven as a place of service. That is very true. But to the working-man, to the man who toils with his brain or with his hands, it must ever be a sweet thought that there is a land where we shall rest. Soon, this voice will never be strained again: soon, these lungs will never have to exert themselves beyond their power; soon, this brain shall not be racked for thought; but I shall sit at the banquet-table of God; yea, I shall recline on the bosom of Abraham, and be at ease for ever. Oh! weary sons and daughters of

Adam, you will not have to drive the ploughshare into the unthankful soil in heaven, you will not need to rise to daily toils before the sun has risen, and labor still when the sun hath long ago gone to his rest; but ye shall be still, ye shall be quiet, ye shall rest yourselves, for all are rich in heaven, all are happy there, all are peaceful. Toil, trouble, travail, and labor are words that cannot be spelled in heaven; they have no such things there, for they always rest.

## The Heavenly Company

And mark the *good company they sit with*. They are to "sit down with Abraham, and Isaac, and Jacob." Some people think that in heaven we shall know nobody. But our text declares here, that we "shall sit down with Abraham, and Isaac, and Jacob." Then I am sure that we shall be aware that they are Abraham, and Isaac, and Jacob. I have heard of a good woman, who asked her husband, when she was dying, "My dear, do you think you will know me when you and I get to heaven?" "Shall I know you?" he said, "why, I have always known you while I have been here, and do you think I shall be a greater fool when I get to heaven?" I think it was a very good answer. If we have known one another here, we shall know one another there. I have dear departed friends up there, and it is always a sweet thought to me, that when I shall put my foot, as I hope I may, upon the threshold of heaven, there will come my sisters and brothers to clasp me by the hand, and say, "Yes, thou lovedst one, and thou art here."

Dear relatives that have been separated, you will meet again in heaven. One of you has lost a mother—she is gone above; and if you follow the track of Jesus, you shall meet her there. Methinks I see yet another coming to meet you at the door of paradise; and though the ties of natural affection may be in a measure forgotten—I may be allowed to use a figure—how blessed would she be as she turned to God, and said, "Here I am, and the children that thou hast given me." We shall recognize our friends:—husband, you will know your wife again. Mother, you will know those dear babes of yours—you marked their features when they lay panting and gasping for breath. You know how ye hung over their graves when the cold sod was sprinkled over them, and it was said, "Earth to earth, dust to dust, and ashes to ashes." But ye shall hear those loved voices again; ye shall hear those sweet voices once more; ye shall yet know that those whom ye loved have been loved by God.

Would not that be a dreary heaven for us to inhabit, where we should be alike unknowing and unknown? I would not care to go to such a heaven as that. I believe that heaven is a fellowship of the saints, and that we shall know one another there. I have often thought I should love to see Isaiah; and, as soon as I get to heaven, methinks, I would ask for him, because he spoke more of Jesus Christ than all the rest. I am sure I should want to find out George Whitefield—he who so continually preached to the people, and wore himself out with a more than seraphic zeal. O yes! we shall have choice company in heaven when we get there. There will be no distinction of learned and unlearned, clergy and laity, but we shall walk freely one among another; we shall feel that we are brethren; we shall "sit down with Abraham, and Isaac, and Jacob."

I have heard of a lady who was visited by a minister on

her deathbed, and she said to him, "I want to ask you one question, now I am about to die." "Well," said the minister, "what is it?" "Oh!" said she, in a very affected way, "I want to know if there are two places in heaven, because I could not bear that Betsy in the kitchen should be in heaven along with me, she is so unrefined." The minister turned round and said, "O, don't trouble yourself about that, madam. There is no fear of that; for until you get rid of your accursed pride, you will never enter heaven at all." We must all get rid of our pride. We must come down and stand on an equality in the sight of God, and see in every man a brother, before we can hope to be found in glory. Ay, we bless God, we thank him that will set down no separate table for one and for another. The Jew and the Gentile will sit down together. The great and the small shall feed in the same pasture, and we shall "sit down with Abraham, and Isaac, and Jacob, in the kingdom of heaven."

But my text hath a yet greater depth of sweetness, for it says, that "*many* shall come and shall sit down." Some narrow-minded bigots think that heaven will be a very small place, where there will be a very few people, who went to their chapel or their church. I confess, I have no wish for a very small heaven, and love to read in the Scriptures that there are many mansions in my Father's house. How often do I hear people say, "Ah! strait is the gate and narrow is the way, and few there be that find it. There will be very few in heaven; there will be most lost." My friend I differ from you. Do you think that Christ will let the devil beat him? that he will let the devil have more in hell than there will be in heaven? No: it is impossible. For then Satan would laugh at Christ. There will be more in heaven than there are among the lost. God says, that "there will be a number that no man can number who will be saved;" but he never says that there will be a number that no man can number that will be lost. There will be a host beyond all count who will get into heaven.

What glad tidings for you and for me! for if there are so many to be saved why should not I be saved? why should not you? why should not yon man, over there in the crowd, say, "Cannot I be one among the multitude?" And may not that poor woman there take heart, and say, "Well, if there were but half-a-dozen saved, I might fear that I should not be one; but since many are to come, why should not I also be saved?" Cheer up, disconsolate! Cheer up, son of mourning, child of sorrow, there is hope for thee still! I can never know that any man is past God's grace. There be a few that have sinned that sin that is unto death and God gives them up; but the vast host of mankind are yet within the reach of sovereign mercy— "And many of them shall come from the east, and from the west, and shall sit down in the kingdom of heaven."

Look at my text again, and you will see where these people come from. They are to "come from the east and west." The Jews said that they would all come from Palestine, every one of them, every man, woman, and child; that there would not be one in heaven that was not a Jew. And the Pharisees thought that if they were not all Pharisees they could not be saved. But Jesus Christ said there will be many that will come from the east and from the west. There will be a multitude from that far off land of China, for God is doing a great work there, and we hope that the gospel will yet be victorious in that land. There will be a multitude from this western land of England; from the western country beyond the sea, in

America; and from the south, in Australia; and from the north, in Canada, Siberia, and Russia. From the uttermost parts of the earth there shall come many to sit down in the kingdom of God.

But I do not think this text is to be understood so much geographically as spiritually. When it says that they "shall come from the east and west," I think it does not refer to nations particularly, but to different kinds of people. Now, "the east and the west" signify those who are the very furthest off from religion; yet many of them will be saved and get to heaven. There is a class of persons who will always be looked upon as hopeless. Many a time have I heard a man or woman say of such a one, "He cannot be saved: he is too abandoned. What is *he* good for? Ask *him* to go to a place of worship—he was drunk on Saturday night. What would be the use of reasoning with *him?* There is no hope for him. He is a hardened fellow. See what he has done these many years. What good will it be to speak to him?"

Now, hear this, ye who think your fellows worse than yourselves—ye who condemn others, whereas ye are often just as guilty: Jesus Christ says "many shall come from the east and west." There will be many in heaven that were drunkards once. I believe, among that blood-bought throng, there are many who reeled in and out the tavern half their lifetime. But by the power of divine grace they were able to dash the liquor cup to the ground. They renounced the riot of intoxication—fled away from it—and served God. Yes! There will be many in heaven who were drunkards on earth. There will be many harlots: some of the most abandoned will be found there.

You remember the story of Whitefield's once saying

that there would be some in heaven who were "the dev-il's castaways"; some that the devil would hardly think good enough for him, and yet whom Christ would save. Lady Huntingdon once gently hinted that such language was not quite proper. But just at the time there happened to be heard come a ring at the bell and Whitefield went down stairs. Afterwards he came up and said, "Your ladyship, what do you think a poor woman had to say to me just now? She was a sad profligate and she said, 'O, Mr. Whitefield, when you were preaching you told us that Christ would take in the devil's castaways and I am one of them,'" and that was the means of her salvation.

Shall anybody ever check us from preaching to the lowest of the low? I have been accused of getting all the rabble of London around me. God bless the rabble! God save the rabble! then, say I. But suppose they are "the rabble"! Who need the gospel more than they do? Who require to have Christ preached to them more than they do? We have lots of those who preach to ladies and gen-tlemen and we want someone to preach to the rabble in these degenerate days. Oh! here is comfort for me, for many of the rabble are to come from the east and from the west.

Oh! what would you think if you were to see the differ-ence between some that are in heaven and some that shall be there! there might be found one whose hair hangs across his eyes, his locks are matted, he looks hor-rible, his bloated eyes start from his face, he grins al-most like an idiot, he has drunk away his very brain until life seems to have departed so far as sense and being are concerned; yet I would tell you, "that man is capable of salvation"—and in a few years I might say "look up yon-der;" see you that bright star? discern you that man with

71

a crown of pure gold upon his head? do you notice that being clad in robes of sapphire and in garments of light? That is the selfsame man who sat there a poor benighted, almost idiotic being; yet sovereign grace and mercy have saved him! There are none, except those as I have said before, who have sinned the unpardonable sin, who are beyond God's mercy—fetch me out the worst, and still I would preach the gospel to them; fetch me out the vilest, still I would preach to them, because I recollect my master said, "Go ye out into the highways and hedges and compel them to come in that my house may be filled." "Many shall come from the east and west, and shall sit down with Abraham, and Isaac, and Jacob, in the kingdom of heaven."

## They Shall Come

There is one more word I must notice before I have done with this sweet portion—that is the word *"shall."* Oh! I love God's "shalls" and "wills." There is nothing comparable to them. Let a man say "shall," what is it good for? "I will," says man, and he never performs; "I shall," says he, and he breaks his promise. But it is never so with God's "shalls." If he says, "shall," it shall be; when he says, "will," it will be. Now he has said here, "many *shall* come." The devil says, "they shall not come;" but "they shall come." Their sins say, "you can't come;" God says, you "shall come." You, yourselves, say, "we won't come;" God says, "you shall come."

Yes! there are some here who are laughing at salvation, who can scoff at Christ, and mock at the gospel; but I tell you some of you shall come yet. "What!" you say, "can God make me become a Christian?" I tell you yes, for herein rests the power of the gospel. It does not ask your consent; but it gets it. It does not say, will you have it, but it makes you willing in the day of God's power. Not against your will, but it makes you willing. It shows you its value, and then you fall in love with it, and straight-way you run after it and have it. Many people have said, "we will not have anything to do with religion," yet they have been converted.

I have heard of a man who once went to chapel to hear the singing, and as soon as the minister began to preach, he put his fingers in his ears and would not listen. But by-and-by some tiny insect settled on his face, so that he was obliged to take one finger out of his ear to brush it away. Just then the minister said, "he that hath ears to hear, let him hear." The man listened; and God met with him at that moment to his soul's conversion. He went out a new man, a changed character. He who came in to laugh retired to pray; he who came in to mock went out to bend his knee in penitence: he who entered to spend an idle hour went home to spend an hour in devotion with his God. The sinner became a saint; the profligate became a penitent.

Who knows that there may not be some like that here? The gospel wants not your consent, it gets it. It knocks the enmity out of your heart. You say "I do not want to be saved;" Christ says you shall be. He makes your will turn round, and then you cry, "Lord, save, or I perish." Ah, might heaven exclaim, "I knew I would make you say that;" and then he rejoices over you because he has changed your will and made you willing in the day of his power. If Jesus Christ were to stand on this platform to-night, what would many people do with him? "O!" say some, "we would make him a king." I do not believe it.

They would crucify him again if they had the opportunity. If he were to come and say, "Here I am, I love you, will you be saved by me?" Not one of you would consent if you were left to your will. If he should look upon you with those eyes, before whose power the lion would have crouched, if he spoke with that voice which poured forth a cataract of eloquence like a stream of nectar rolling down from the cliffs above, not a single person would come to be his disciple; no, it wants the power of the Spirit to make men come to Jesus Christ.

He himself said, "No man can come to me except the Father who hath sent me draw him." Ah! we want that; and here we have it. They shall come! They shall come! ye may laugh, ye may despise us; but Jesus Christ shall not die for nothing. If some of you reject him there are some that will not. If there are some that are not saved, others *shall* be. Christ *shall* see his seed, he *shall* prolong his days, and the pleasure of the Lord *shall* prosper in his hands. Some think that Christ died and yet that some for whom he died will be lost. I never could understand that doctrine. If Jesus my surety bore my griefs and carried my sorrows, I believe myself to be as secure as the angels in heaven. God cannot ask payment twice. If Christ paid my debt shall I have to pay it again? No.

> Free from sin I walk at large,
> The Saviour's blood's my full discharge;
> At his dear feet content I lay,
> A sinner saved, and homage pay.

They shall come! They shall come! And nought in heaven, nor on earth, nor in hell, can stop them from coming.

And now, thou chief of sinners, list one moment while I call thee to Jesus. There is one person here to-night who thinks himself the worst soul that ever lived. There is one who says to himself, "I do not deserve to be called to Christ I am sure!" Soul! I call thee! thou lost, most wretched outcast, this night, by authority given me of God, I call thee to come to my Savior. Some time ago, when I went into the County Court to see what they were doing, I heard a man's name called out, and immediately the man said, "Make way! make way! they call me!" And up he came. Now, I call the chief of sinners to-night, and let him say, "Make way! Make way doubts! Make way fears! Make way sins! Christ calls me! And if Christ calls me, that is enough!"

> I'll to his gracious feet approach
>     Whose sceptre mercy gives;
> Perhaps he may command my touch!
>     And then the suppliant lives.
>
> I can but perish if I go;
>     I am resolved to try;
> For if I stay away, I know
>     I must for ever die.
>
> But, should I die with mercy sought,
>     When I the King have tried,
> That were to die, (delightful thought!)
>     As sinner never died.

Go and try my Savior! Go and try my Savior! If he casts you away after you have sought him, tell it in the pit that Christ would not hear you. But *that* you shall never be allowed to do. It would dishonor the mercy of the covenant, for God to cast away one penitent sinner; and it never shall be while it is written "many shall come from the east and west, and shall sit down with Abraham, and Isaac, and Jacob, in the kingdom of heaven."

The second part of my text is heart-breaking. I could preach with great delight to myself from the first part; but here is a dreary task to my soul, because there are gloomy words here. But, as I have told you, what is written in the Bible must be preached whether it be gloomy or cheerful. There are some ministers who never mention anything about hell. I heard of a minister who once said to his congregation—"If you do not love the Lord Jesus Christ you will be sent to that place which it is not polite to mention." He ought not to have been allowed to preach again, I am sure, if he could not use plain words. Now, if I saw that house on fire over there, do you think I would stand and say, "I believe the operation of combustion is proceeding yonder!" No; I would call out, "Fire! Fire!" and then everybody would know what I meant.

## Children of the Kingdom Cast Out

So, if the Bible says, "The children of the kingdom shall be cast out into outer darkness," am I to stand here and mince the matter at all? God forbid. We must speak the truth as it is written. It is a terrible truth, for it says, "*the children of the kingdom* shall be cast out!" Now, who are those children? I will tell you—"The children of the kingdom" are those people who are noted for the externals of piety, but who have nothing of the internals it. People whom you will see with their Bibles and Hymn Books marching off to chapel as religiously as possible, or going to church as devoutly and demurely as they can, looking as somber and serious as parish beadles, and fancying that they are quite sure to be saved, though their heart is not in the matter, nothing but their bodies. These are the persons who are "the children of the kingdom." They have no grace, no life, no Christ, and they shall be cast into outer darkness.

Again, these people are *the children of pious fathers and mothers*. There is nothing touches a man's heart, mark you, like talking about his mother. I have heard of a swearing sailor, whom nobody could manage, not even the police, who was always making some disturbance wherever he went. Once he went into a place of worship, and no one could keep him still; but a gentleman went up and said to him, "Jack, you had a mother once." With that the tears ran down his cheeks. He said, "Ha! bless you, sir, I had; and I brought her grey hairs with sorrow to the grave, and a pretty fellow I am to be here to-night." He then sat down, quite sobered and subdued by the very mention of his mother.

Ah! and there are some of you "children of the kingdom" who can remember your mothers. Your mother took you on her knee and taught you early to pray: your father tutored you in the ways of godliness. And yet you are here to-night without grace in your heart—without hope of heaven. You are going downwards towards hell as fast as your feet can carry you. There are some of you who have broken your poor mother's heart. Oh! if I could tell you what she has suffered for you when you have at night been indulging in your sin. Do you know what your guilt will be, ye "children of the kingdom," if ye perish after a pious mother's prayers and tears have fallen upon you? I can conceive of no one entering hell with a worse grace than the man who goes there with drops of his mother's tears on his head, and with his father's prayers following him at his heels.

Some of you will inevitably endure this doom, some of

you young men and women shall wake up one day and find yourselves in outer darkness, while your parents shall be up there in heaven, looking down upon you with upbraiding eyes, seeming to say, "What! after all we did for you, all we said, are ye come to this?" "Children of the kingdom!" do not think that a pious mother can save you. Do not think because your father was a member of such-and-such a church that his godliness will save you. I can suppose some one standing at heaven's gate and demanding, "Let me in! Let me in!" What for? "Because my mother is in there." Your mother had nothing to do with you. If she was holy, she was holy for herself; if she was evil, she was evil for herself. "But my grandfather prayed for me." That is no use: Did you pray for yourself? "No; I did not." Then grandfathers' prayers and grandmothers' prayers, and fathers' and mothers' prayers, may be piled on the top of one another till they reach the stars, but they never can make a ladder for you to go to heaven by. You must seek God for yourself; or rather God must seek you. You must have vital experience of godliness in your heart, or else you are lost, even though all your friends were in heaven.

That was a dreadful dream which a pious mother once had, and told to her children. She thought the judgment-day was come. The great books were opened. They all stood before God. And Jesus Christ said, "Separate the chaff from the wheat; put the goats on the left hand, and the sheep on the right." The mother dreamed that she and her children were standing just in the middle of the great assembly. And the angel came, and said, "I must take the mother: she is a sheep: she must go to the right hand. The children are goats: they must go on the left." She thought as she went her children clutched her, and said, "Mother, can we part? Must we be separated?" She then put her arms around them, and seemed to say, "My children, I would, if possible, take you with me." But in a moment the angel touched her: her cheeks were dried, and, now, overcoming natural affection, being rendered supernatural and sublime, resigned to God's will, she said, "My children, I taught you well, I trained you up, and you forsook the ways of God, and now all I have to say is, Amen to your condemnation." Thereupon they were snatched away, and she saw them in perpetual torment, while she was in heaven.

Young man, what will you think, when the last day comes, to hear Christ say, "Depart, ye cursed!" And there will be a voice just behind him, saying, Amen. And as you inquire whence came the voice, you will find it was your mother. Or, young woman, when thou art cast away into outer darkness, what will you think to hear a voice saying, Amen. And as you look, there sits your father, his lips still moving with the solemn curse. "Ah! children of the kingdom," the penitent reprobates will enter heaven, many of them; publicans and sinners will get there; repenting drunkards and swearers will be saved; but many of "the children of the kingdom" will be cast out. Oh! to think that you who have been so well trained should be lost, while many of the worse will be saved. It will be the hell of hell for you to look up and see there "poor Jack" the drunkard lying in Abraham's bosom, while you who have had a pious mother are cast into hell, simply because you would not believe on the Lord Jesus Christ, but put his gospel from you, and lived and died without it! That were the very sting of all, to see ourselves cast away, when the chief of sinners finds salvation.

## They Shall Be Cast Out

Now list to me a little while—I will not detain you long—whilst I undertake the doleful task of telling you what is to become of these "children of the kingdom." Jesus Christ says, they are to be "cast into outer darkness, where there is weeping and gnashing of teeth."

First, notice, they are to be *cast out*. They are not said to *go;* but when they come to heaven's gates they are to be *cast* out. As soon as hypocrites arrive at the gates of heaven, Justice will say, "There he comes! there he comes! he spurned a father's prayers, and mocked a mother's tears. He has forced his way downward against all the advantages mercy has supplied. And now, there he comes. Gabriel, take the man." The angel binding you hand and foot, holds you one single moment over the mouth of the chasm. He bids you look down—down—down. There is no bottom: and you hear coming up from the abyss, "sullen moans, and hollow groans, and shrieks of tortured ghosts." You quiver, your bones melt like wax, and your marrow quakes within you. Where is now thy might? and where thy boasting and bragging? Ye shriek and cry, ye beg for mercy; but the angel with one tremendous grasp, seizes you fast, and then hurls you down, with the cry, "Away, away!" And down you go to the pit that is bottomless, and roll for ever downward—downward—downward—ne'er to find a resting-place for the sole of your foot. Ye shall be cast out.

And *where are you to be cast to?* Ye are to be cast "into outer darkness;" ye are to be put in the place where there will be no hope. For, by "light," in Scripture, we understand "hope;" and you are to be put "into outer darkness," where there is no light—no hope. Is there a man here who has no hope? I cannot suppose such a person. One of you, perhaps, says, "I am thirty pounds in debt, and shall be sold up by-and-by; but I have a hope that I may get a loan, and so escape my difficulty." Says another, "My business is ruined, but things may take a turn yet—I have a hope." Says another, "I am in great distress, but I hope that God will provide for me." Another says, "I am fifty pounds in debt; I am sorry for it: but I will set these strong hands to work, and do my best to get out of it." One of you thinks a friend is dying; but you have a hope that perhaps the fever may take a turn— that he may yet live.

But, in hell, there is no hope. They have not even the hope of dying—the hope of being annihilated. They are for ever—for ever—for ever—lost! On every chain in hell, there is written "for ever." In the fires, there, blaze out the words, "for ever." Up above their heads, they read, "for ever." Their eyes are galled, and their hearts are pained with the thought that it is "for ever." Oh! if I could tell you to-night that hell would one day be burned out, and that those who were lost might be saved, there would be a jubilee in hell at the very thought of it. But it cannot be—it is *"for ever"* they are "cast into outer darkness."

But I want to get over this as quickly as I can, for who can bear to talk thus to his fellow creatures? What is it that the lost are doing? They are "weeping and gnashing their teeth." Do you gnash your teeth now? You would not do it except you were in pain and agony. Well, in hell there is always gnashing of teeth. And do you know why? There is one gnashing his teeth at his companion, and mutters—"I was led into hell by you; you led me astray, you taught me to drink the first time." And the other gnashes his teeth and says, "What if I did, you made me worse than I should have been in after times." There is a child who looks at her mother, and says, "Mother, you trained me up to vice." And the mother gnashes her teeth again at the child, and says, "I have no pity for you, for you excelled me in it and led me into deeper sin." Fathers gnash their teeth at their sons, and sons at their fathers.

And, methinks, if there are any who will have to gnash their teeth more than others, it will be seducers, when they see those whom they have led from the paths of virtue, and hear them saying, "Ah! we are glad you are in hell with us, you deserve it, for you led us here." Have any of you, to-night, upon your consciences the fact that you have led others to the pit? O may sovereign grace forgive you. "We have gone astray like lost sheep," said David. Now, a lost sheep never goes astray alone if it is one of a flock. I lately read of a sheep that leaped over the parapet of a bridge, and was followed by every one of the flock. So if one man goes astray he leads others with him. Some of you will have to account for others' sins when you get to hell, as well as your own. Oh, what "weeping and gnashing of teeth" there will be in that pit!

## A Final Warning and Plea

Now shut the black book. Who wants to say any more about it? I have warned you solemnly. I have told you of the wrath to come! The evening darkens, and the sun is setting. Ah! and the evenings darken with some of you. I can see grey-headed men here. Are your grey hairs a crown of glory or a fool's cap to you? Are you on the very verge of heaven, or are you tottering on the brink of your grave, and sinking down to perdition?

Let me warn you, grey-headed men; your evening is coming. O poor tottering grey-head, wilt thou take the last step into the pit? Let a young child step before thee and beg thee to consider. There is thy staff—it has nothing of earth to rest upon; and now, ere thou diest, bethink thyself this night; let seventy years of sin start up; let the ghosts of thy forgotten transgressions march before thine eyes. What wilt thou do with seventy wasted years to answer for, with seventy years of criminality to bring before God? God give thee grace this night to repent and to put thy trust in Jesus.

And you middle-aged men are not safe: the evening lowers with you too; you may soon die. A few mornings ago, I was roused early from my bed, by the request that I would hasten to see a dying man. I hurried off with all speed to see the poor creature; but when I reached the house he was dead—a corpse. As I stood in the room, I thought, "Ah! that man little thought he should die so soon." There were his wife and children and friends— they little thought he should die, for he was hale, strong, and hearty but a few days before. None of you have a lease of your lives. If you have, where is it? Go and see if you have it anywhere in your chests at home. No! ye may die to-morrow. Let me therefore warn you by the mercy of God; let me speak to you as a brother may speak; for I love you, you know I do, and would press the matter home to your hearts. Oh to be amongst the many who shall be accepted in Christ—how blessed that will be! And God has said that whosoever shall call on his name shall be saved: he casts out none that come unto him through Christ.

And now, ye youths and maidens, one word with you. Perhaps ye think that religion is not for you. "Let us be happy," say you: "let us be merry and joyous." How long, young man, how long? "Till I am twenty-one." Are you sure that you will live till then? Let me tell you one thing. If you do live till that time, if you have no heart for God now, you will have none then. Men do not get better if left alone. It is with them as with a garden: if you let it alone, and permit weeds to grow, you will not expect to find it better in six months—but worse. Ah! men talk as if they could repent when they like. It is the work of God to give us repentance. Some even say, "I shall turn to God on such-and-such a day." Ah! If you felt aright, you would say, "I must run to God, and ask him to give me repentance now; lest I should die before I have found Jesus Christ my Savior."

Now one word in conclusion. I have told you of heaven and hell; what is the way, then, to escape from hell and to be found in heaven? I will not tell you my old tale again to-night. I recollect when I told it you before, a good friend in the crowd said, "Tell us something fresh old fellow." Now really in preaching ten times a week, we cannot always say things fresh. You have heard John Gough, and you know he tells his tales over again. I have nothing but the old gospel. "He that believeth and is baptized shall be saved." There is nothing here of works. It does not say "He who is a good man shall be saved," but "he who believes and is baptized."

Well, what is it to believe? It is to put your trust entirely upon Jesus. Poor Peter once believed, and Jesus Christ said to him, "Come on, Peter, walk to me on the water." Peter went stepping along on the tops of the waves without sinking; but when he looked at the waves, he began to tremble, and down he went. Now, poor sinner, Christ says, "Come on; walk on in your sins; come to me;" and if you do, he will give you power. If you believe on Christ, you will be able to walk over your sins—to tread upon them, and overcome them.

I can remember the time when my sins first stared me in the face. I thought myself the most accursed of all men. I had not committed any very great open transgressions against God; but I recollected that I had been well trained and tutored, and I thought my sins were thus greater than other people's. I cried to God to have mercy, but I feared that he would not pardon me. Month after month I cried to God, but he did not hear me, and I knew not what it was to be saved. Sometimes I was so weary of the world that I desired to die: but then I recollected that there was a worse world after this, and that it would be an ill matter to rush before my Maker unprepared. At times I wickedly thought God a most heartless tyrant, because he did not answer my prayer; and then, at others, I thought, "I deserve his displeasure; if he sends me to hell, he will be just."

But I remember the hour when I stepped into a place of worship, and saw a tall thin man step into the pulpit: I have never seen him from that day, and probably never shall, till we meet in heaven. He opened the Bible, and read, with a feeble voice, "Look unto me and be ye saved, all the ends of the earth; for I am God, and beside him there is none else." Ah! thought I, I am one of the ends of the earth; and then, turning round, and fixing his gaze on me, as if he knew me, the minister said, "Look, look, look." Why, I thought I had a great deal to *do*, but I found

85

it was only to *look*. I thought I had a garment to spin out for myself: but I found that if I looked, Christ would give me a garment.

Look, sinner, that is to be saved. Look unto him all ye ends of the earth, and be saved. This is what the Jews did, when Moses held up the brazen serpent. He said, "Look!" and they looked. The serpents might be twisting round them, and they might be nearly dead; but they simply looked, and the moment they looked, the serpents dropped off, and they were healed. Look to Jesus, sinner. "None but Jesus can do helpless sinners good." There is a hymn we often sing, but which I do not think is quite right, it says,

> Venture on him, venture wholly;
> Let no other trust intrude.

Now, it is no venture to trust in Christ, not in the least. He who trusts in Christ is quite secure. I recollect that when dear John Hyatt was dying, Matthew Wilks said to him, in his usual tone, "Well, John, could you trust your soul in the hands of Jesus Christ now?" "Yes," said he, "a million! a million souls!" I am sure that every Christian that has ever trusted in Christ can say, "Amen" to that. Trust in him; he will never deceive you. My blessed Master will never cast you away.

I cannot speak much longer, and I have only to thank you for your kindness. I never saw so large a number so still and quiet. I really think, after all the hard things that have been said, that the English people know who loves them, and that they will stand by the man who stands by them. I thank every one of you, and above all, I beg you, if there be reason or sense in what I have said, bethink yourselves of what you are, and may the blessed Spirit reveal to you your state! May he show you that you are dead, that you are lost, ruined. May he make you feel what a dreadful thing it would be to sink into hell! May he point you to heaven! May he take you as the angel did of old, and put his hand upon you, and say, "Flee! flee! flee! Look to the mountain; look not behind thee; stay not in all the plain." And may we all meet in heaven at last; and there we shall be happy for ever.

*One of Spurgeon's most reprinted sermons is "Songs in the Night," which was delivered early in his career at the New Park Street Baptist Church. "Any man can sing in the day," Spurgeon says. But the one who has faith in God can sing songs in the night because God Himself is the author and subject of his songs. Spurgeon finds that such songs, impossible for natural man, are "one of the best arguments in all the world in favor of your religion." Throughout most of the sermon Spurgeon addresses the children of God, but he turns to sinners in his conclusion, as was his custom, and concludes by warning that there is a night coming in which there will be no songs of joy.*

## CHAPTER FOUR

# *Songs in the Night*

*But none saith, Where is God my Maker, who giveth songs in the night? (Job 35:10).*

Elihu was a wise man, exceedingly wise, though not as wise as the all-wise Jehovah, who sees light in the clouds, and finds order in confusion; hence Elihu, being much puzzled at beholding Job so afflicted, cast about him to find the cause of it, and he very wisely hit upon one of the most likely reasons, although it did not happen to be the right one in Job's case. He said within himself, "Surely, if men are sorely tried and troubled, it is because, while they think about their troubles, and distress themselves about their fears, they do not say, 'Where is God my Maker, who giveth songs in the night?'" Elihu's reason is right in the majority of cases. The great cause of a Christian's distress, the reason of the depths of sorrow into which many believers are plunged, is simply this—that while they are looking about, on the right hand and on the left, to see how they may escape their troubles, they forget to look to the hills whence all real help cometh; they do not say, "Where is God my Maker, who giveth songs in the night?"

We shall, however, leave that enquiry, and dwell upon those sweet words, "God my Maker, who giveth songs in the night." The world hath its night. It seemeth necessary that it should have one. The sun shineth by day, and men go forth to their labors; but they grow weary, and nightfall cometh on, like a sweet boon from heaven. The darkness draweth the curtains, and shutteth out the light, which might prevent our eyes from slumber; while the sweet, calm stillness of the night permits us to rest upon the bed of ease, and there forget awhile our cares, until the morning sun appeareth, and an angel puts his hand upon the curtain, undraws it once again, touches our eyelids, and bids us rise, and proceed to the labors of the day. Night is one of the greatest blessings men enjoy; we have many reasons to thank God for it.

Yet night is to many a gloomy season. There is "the pestilence that walketh in darkness;" there is "the terror by night"; there is the dread of robbers and of fell disease, with all those fears that the timorous know, when they have no light wherewith they can discern different objects. It is then they fancy that spiritual creatures walk the earth; though, if they knew rightly, they would find it to be true that—

> Millions of spiritual creatures walk the earth
> Unseen, both when we wake, and when we sleep,—

and that at all times they are round about us, not more by night than by day.

Night is the season of terror and alarm to most men; yet even night hath its songs. Have you never stood by the seaside at night, and heard the pebbles sing, and the waves chant God's praises? Or have you never risen from your couch, and thrown up the window of your chamber, and listened there? Listened to what? Silence—save now and then a murmuring sound, which seems sweet music then. And have you not fancied that you have heard the harps of gold playing in heaven? Did you not conceive that yon stars—those eyes of God, looking down on you, were also mouths of song, that every star was singing God's glory, singing as it shone its mighty Maker's well-deserved praise? Night hath its songs; we need not much poetry in our spirit to catch the song of night, and hear the spheres as they chant praises which are loud to the heart, though they be silent to the ear,—the praises of the mighty God, who bears up the unpillared arch of heaven, and moves the stars in their courses.

Man, too, like the great world in which he lives, must have his night. For it is true that man is like the world around him; he is himself a little world; he resembles the world in almost everything; and if the world hath its night, so hath man. And many a night do we have,—nights of sorrow, nights of persecution, nights of doubt, nights of bewilderment, nights of affliction, nights of anxiety, nights of ignorance, nights of all kinds, which press upon our spirits, and terrify our souls. But blessed be God, the Christian man can say, "My God giveth me songs in the night."

It is not necessary, I take it, to prove to you that Christian men have nights; for if you are Christians, you will find that *you* have them, and you will not want any proof, for nights will come quite often enough. I will, therefore, proceed at once to the subject; and notice, with regard to songs in the night, first, *their source*, God giveth them; secondly, *their matter*,—what do we sing about in the night? Thirdly, *their excellence*,—they are hearty songs, and they are sweet ones; and fourthly, *their uses*, their benefits to ourselves and others.

## The Author of Our Songs in the Night

I. First, songs in the night—WHO IS THE AUTHOR OF THEM? *"God,"* says the text, our "Maker, giveth songs in the night."

Any man can sing in the day. When the cup is full, man draws inspiration from it; when wealth rolls in abundance around him, any man can sing to the praise of a God who gives a plenteous harvest, or sends home a loaded argosy. It is easy enough for an Aeolian harp to whisper music when the winds blow; the difficulty is for music to come when no wind bloweth. It is easy to sing when we can read the notes by daylight; but he is the skilful singer who can sing when there is not a ray of light by which to read,—who sings from his heart, and not from a book that he can see, because he has no means of reading, save from that inward book of his own living spirit, whence notes of gratitude pour forth in songs of praise.

No man can make a song in the night himself; he may attempt it, but he will find how difficult it is. It is not natural to sing in trouble, "Bless the Lord, O my soul, and all that is within me bless his holy name," for that is a daylight song. But it was a divine song which Habakkuk sang when in the night he said, "Although the fig-tree shall not blossom," and so on, "yet I will rejoice in the Lord, I will joy in the God of my salvation." Methinks, on the margin of the Red Sea, any man could have made a song like that of Moses, "The horse and his rider hath he thrown into the sea;" the difficulty would have been to compose a song before the Red Sea had been divided, and to sing it before Pharaoh's hosts had been drowned, while yet the darkness of doubt and fear was resting on Israel's hosts. Songs in the night come only from God; they are not in the power of man.

But what does the text mean, when it asserts that God giveth songs in the night? We think we find two answers to the question. The first is, that usually in the night of a Christian's experience, *God is his only song*. If it be daylight in my heart, I can sing songs touching my graces, songs touching my sweet experiences, songs touching my duties, songs touching my labors; but let the night come, my graces appear to have withered; my evidences, though they are there, are hidden; now I have nothing left to sing of but my God. It is strange that, when God gives his children mercies, they generally set their hearts more on the mercies than on the Giver of them; but when the night comes, and he sweeps all the mercies away, then at once they each say, "Now, my God, I have nothing to sing of but thee; I must come to thee, and to thee only. I had cisterns once; they were full of water; I drank from them then; but now the created streams are dry, sweet Lord, I quaff no stream but thine own self, I drink from no fount but from thee."

Ay, child of God, thou knowest what I say; or if thou dost not understand it yet, thou wilt do so by-and-by! It is in the night we sing of God, and of God alone. Every string is tuned, and every power hath its tribute of song, while we praise God, and nothing else. We can sacrifice to ourselves in daylight; we only sacrifice to God by night. We can sing high praises to ourselves when all is joyful; but we cannot sing praise to any save our God when circumstances are untoward, and providences appear adverse. God alone can furnish us with songs in the night.

And yet again, not only does God give the song in the night, because he is the only subject upon which we can sing then, but because *he is the only One who inspires songs in the night*. Bring me a poor, melancholy, distressed child of God; I seek to tell him precious promises, and whisper to him sweet words of comfort; he listeneth not to me, he is like the deaf adder, he heeds not the voice of the charmer, charm he never so wisely. Send him round to all the comforting divines, and all the holy Barnabases who ever preached, and they will do very little with him; they will not be able to squeeze a song out of him, do what they may. He is drinking the gall and wormwood; he says, "O Lord, I have eaten ashes like bread, and mingled my drink with weeping;" and comfort him as you may, it will be only a woeful note or two of mournful resignation that you will get from him; you will evoke no psalms of praise, no hallelujahs, no joyful sonnets.

But let God come to his child in the night, let him whisper in his ear as he lies on his bed, and now you can see his eyes glisten in the night season. Do you not hear him say,—

> 'Tis Paradise, if thou art here;
> If thou depart, 'tis hell?

*I* could not have cheered him: it is God that has done it; for God "giveth songs in the night." It is marvellous, brethren, how one sweet word of God will make many songs for Christians. One word of God is like a piece of gold, and the Christian is the gold-beater, and he can hammer that promise out for whole weeks. I can say myself, I have lived on one promise for weeks, and wanted no other. I had just simply to hammer the promise out into gold-leaf, and plate my whole existence with joy from it. The Christian gets his songs from God; God gives him inspiration, and teaches him how to sing: "God my Maker, who giveth songs in the night." So, then, poor Christian, thou needest not go pumping up thy poor heart to make it glad. Go to thy Maker, and ask him to give thee a song in the night; for thou art a poor dry well. You have heard it said that, when a pump is dry, you must pour water down it first of all, and then you will get some up. So, Christian, when thou art dry, go to thy God, ask him to pour some joy down thee, and then thou wilt get more joy up from thine own heart. Do not go to this comforter or that, for you will find them "Job's comforters" after all; but go thou first and foremost to thy Maker, for he is the great Composer of songs and Teacher of music, he it is who can teach thee how to sing.

## The Subject of Our Songs in the Night

II. Thus we have dwelt upon the first point; now turn to the second. WHAT IS GENERALLY THE MATTER CONTAINED IN A SONG IN THE NIGHT? What do we sing about?

Why, I think, when we sing by night, there are three things we sing about. Either we sing about the day that is over, or about the night itself, or else about the morrow that is to come. Those are all sweet themes, when God our Maker gives us songs in the night. In the midst of the night, the most usual method is for Christians to sing about *the day that is over*. The man says, "It is night now, but I can remember when it was daylight. Neither moon nor stars appear at present; but I recollect when I saw the sun. I have no evidences just now; but there was a time when I could say. 'I know that my Redeemer liveth.' I have my doubts and fears at this present moment; but it

97

is not long since I could say with full assurance, 'I know that he shed his blood for me.' It may be darkness now; but I know the promises *were sweet;* I know I had blessed seasons in his house. I am quite sure of this, I used to enjoy myself in the ways of the Lord; and though now my path is strewn with thorns, I know it is the King's highway. It was a way of pleasantness once, it will be a way of pleasantness again. 'I will remember the years of the right hand of the Most High.' "

Christian, perhaps the best song thou canst sing, to cheer thee in the night, is the song of yestermorn. Remember, it was not always night with thee; night is a new thing to thee. Once thou hadst a glad heart and a buoyant spirit; once thine eye was full of fire; once thy foot was light; once thou couldst sing for very joy and ecstasy of heart. Well, then, remember that God who made thee sing yesterday has not left thee in the night. He is not a daylight God who cannot know his children in darkness, but he loves thee now as much as ever; though he has left thee for a little while, it is to prove thee, to make thee trust him better, and love and serve him more. Let me tell you some of the sweet things of which a Christian may make a song when it is night with him.

If we are going to sing of the things of yesterday, let us begin with what God did for us in past times. My beloved brethren, you will find it a sweet subject for song at times to begin to sing of electing love and covenant mercies. When thou thyself art low, it is well to sing of the Fountain-head of mercy, of that blessed decree wherein thou wast ordained unto eternal life, and of that glorious Man who undertook thy redemption; of that solemn covenant signed, and sealed, and ratified, in all things ordered well; of that everlasting love which, ere the hoary mountains were begotten, or ere the aged hills were children, chose thee, loved thee firmly, loved thee fast, loved thee well, loved thee eternally.

I tell thee, believer, if thou canst go back to the years of eternity,—if thou canst in thy mind run back to that period before the everlasting hills were fashioned, or the fountains of the great deep were scooped out, and if thou canst see thy God inscribing thy name in his eternal Book,—if thou canst read in his loving heart eternal thoughts of love to thee, thou wilt find this a charming means of giving thee songs in the night. There are no songs like those which come from electing love, no sonnets like those that are dictated by meditations on discriminating mercy.

Think, Christian, of the eternal covenant, and thou wilt get a song in the night. But if thou hast not a voice tuned to so high a key as that, let me suggest some other mercies thou mayest sing of; they are the mercies thou hast experienced. What, man! canst thou not sing a little of that blessed hour when Jesus met thee, when a blind slave thou wast sporting with death, and he saw thee, and said, "Come, poor slave, come with me"? Canst thou not sing of that rapturous moment when he snapped thy fetters, dashed thy chains to the earth, and said, "I am the Breaker; I am come to break thy chains, and set thee free"? Though thou art ever so gloomy now, canst thou forget that happy morning when, in the house of God, thy voice was loud, almost as a seraph's voice, in praise, for thou couldst sing, "I am forgiven! I am forgiven; a monument of grace, a sinner saved by blood"? Go back, man; sing of that moment, and then thou wilt have a song in the night.

Or, if thou hast almost forgotten that, then surely thou hast some precious milestone along the road of life that is not quite overgrown with moss, on which thou canst read some happy inscription of God's mercy towards thee. What! didst thou never have a sickness like that which thou art suffering now, and did he not raise thee up from it? Wast thou never poor before, and did he not supply thy wants? Wast thou never in straits before, and did he not deliver thee? Come, man! I beseech thee, go to the river of thine experience, and pull up a few bulrushes, and weave them into an ark, wherein thine infant faith may float safely on the stream. I bid thee not forget what God hath done for thee. What! hast thou buried thy diary? I beseech thee, man, turn over the book of thy remembrance. Canst thou not see some sweet hill Mizar? Canst thou not think of some blessed hour when the Lord met with thee at Hermon? Hast thou never been on the Delectable Mountains? Hast thou never been fetched from the den of lions? Hast thou never escaped the jaw of the lion, and the paw of the bear? Nay, O man, I know thou hast! Go back, then, a little way, to the mercies of the past; and though it is dark now, light up the lamps of yesterday, and they shall glitter through the darkness, and thou shalt find that God hath given thee a song in the night.

"Ay!" says one, "but you know that, when we are in the dark, we cannot see the mercies that God has given us. It is all very well for you to talk to us thus, but we cannot get hold of them." I remember an old experimental Christian speaking about the great pillars of our faith; he was a sailor, and we were then on board ship, and there were sundry huge posts on the shore, to which the vessels were usually fastened by throwing a cable over them. After I had told him a great many promises, he said, "I know they are good promises, but I cannot get near enough to shore to throw my cable around them; that is the difficulty." Now, it often happens that God's past mercies and lovingkindnesses would be good sure posts to hold on to, but we have not faith enough to throw our cable around them, so we go slipping down the stream of unbelief, because we cannot stay ourselves by our former mercies.

I will, however, give you something over which I think you can throw your cable. If God has never been kind to you, one thing you surely know, and that is, he has been kind to others. Come, now; if thou art in ever so great straits, surely there have been others in greater straits. What! art thou lower down than poor Jonah was when he went to the bottom of the mountains? Art thou worse off than thy Master when he had not where to lay his head? What! conceivest thou thyself to be the worst of the worst? Look at Job there, scraping himself with a potsherd, and sitting on a dunghill. Art thou as low as he? Yet Job rose up, and was richer than before; and out of the depths Jonah came, and preached the Word; and our Savior Jesus hath mounted to his throne.

O Christian, only think of what God has done for others! If thou canst not recollect that he has done anything for thee, yet remember, I beseech thee, what his usual rule is, and do not judge hardly of my God. You remember when Benhadad was overcome and fled, his servants said to him, "Behold now, we have heard that the kings of the house of Israel are merciful kings; let us, I pray thee, put on sackcloth on our loins, and ropes upon our heads, and go out to the king of Israel: peradventure he will save thy life. So they girded sackcloth on their loins, and put ropes on their heads, and said, Thy servant Benhadad saith, I pray thee, let me live." What said the king? "Is he yet alive? he is my brother." And truly, poor soul, if thou hadst never had a merciful God, yet others have had; the King of kings is merciful; go and try him. If thou art ever so low in thy troubles, look to the hills, from whence cometh thy help. Others have had help therefrom, and so mayest thou. Up might start hundreds of God's children, and show us their hands full of comforts and mercies; and they could say, "The Lord gave us these without money and without price; and why should he not give to thee also, seeing that thou too art the King's son?"

Thus, Christian, thou mayest get a song in the night out of other people, if thou canst not get a song from thyself. Never be ashamed of taking a leaf out of another man's experience book. If thou canst find no good leaf in thine own, tear one out of someone else's; if thou hast no cause to be grateful to God in darkness, or canst not find cause in thine own experience, go to someone else, and, if thou canst, harp God's praise in the dark, and like the nightingale, sing his praise sweetly when all the world has gone to rest; sing in the night of the mercies of yesterday.

But I think, beloved, there is never so dark a night but there is something to sing about, even *concerning that night;* for there is one thing I am sure we can sing about, let the night be ever so dark, and that is, "It is of the Lord's mercies that we are not consumed, and because his compassions fail not." If we cannot sing very loudly, yet we can sing a little low tune, something like this, "He hath not dealt with us after our sins, nor rewarded us according to our iniquities." "Oh!" says one, "I do not know where I shall get my dinner tomorrow; I am a poor wretch." So you may be, my dear friend; but you are not so poor as you deserve to be. Do not be mightily offended about that; if you are, you are no child of God; for the child of God acknowledges that he has no right to the least of God's mercies, but that they come through the channel of grace alone. As long as I am out of hell, I have no right to grumble; and if I were in hell, I should have no right to complain, for I felt, when convinced of sin, that never creature deserved to go there more than I did. We have no cause to murmur; we can lift up our hands, and say, "Night! thou art dark, but thou mightest have been darker. I am poor, but if I could not have been poorer, I might have been sick. I am poor and sick, yet I have some friends left; my lot cannot be so bad but it might have been worse."

Therefore, Christian, you will always have one thing to sing about, "Lord, I thank thee it is not all darkness!" Besides, however dark the night is, there is always a star or moon. There is scarcely a night that we have, but there are just one or two little lamps burning in the sky, and however dark it may be, I think you may find some little comfort, some little joy, some little mercy left, and some little promise to cheer thy spirit. The stars are not put out, are they? Nay, if thou canst not see them, they are there; but methinks one or two must be shining on thee, therefore give God a song in the night. If thou hast only one star, bless God for that one, and perhaps he will make it two; and if thou hast only two stars, bless God twice for the two stars, and perhaps he will make them four. Try, then, if thou canst not find a song in the night.

But, beloved, there is another thing of which we can sing yet more sweetly; and that is, we can sing of *the day that is to come.* Often do I cheer myself with the thought of the coming of the Lord. We preach now, perhaps, with little success; "the kingdoms of this world" have not yet "become the kingdoms of our God and of his Christ." We are laboring, but we do not see the fruit of our labor. Well, what then? We shall not always labor in vain, or spend our strength for nought. A day is coming when every minister of Christ shall speak with unction, when all the servants of God shall preach with power, and when colossal systems of heathenism shall tumble from their pedestals, and mighty, gigantic delusions shall be scattered to the winds. The shout shall be heard, "Alleluia! Alleluia! the Lord God Omnipotent reigneth."

For that day do I look; it is to the bright horizon of Christ's second coming that I turn my eyes. My anxious expectation is, that the blessed Sun of righteousness will soon arise with healing in his wings, that the oppressed shall be righted, that despotism shall be cut down, that liberty shall be established, that peace shall be made lasting, and that the glorious liberty of the children of God shall be extended throughout the known world. Christian! if it is night with thee, think of the morrow; cheer up thy heart with the thought of the coming of thy Lord. Be patient, for you know who has said, "Behold, I come quickly; and my reward is with me, to give every man according as his work shall be."

One thought more upon that point. There is another sweet tomorrow of which we hope to sing in the night. Soon, beloved, you and I shall lie on our dying bed, and we shall not lack a song in the night then: and I do not know where we shall get that song, if we do not get it from the to-morrow. Kneeling by the bed of an apparently dying saint recently, I said, "Well, sister, the Lord has been very precious to you; you can rejoice in his covenant mercies, and his past lovingkindnesses." She put out her hand, and said, "Ah, sir! do not talk about them now; I want the sinner's Savior as much now as ever; it is not a saint's Savior I want, it is still a sinner's Savior that I need, for I am a sinner still." I found that I could not comfort her with the past; so I reminded her of the golden streets, of the gates of pearl, of the walls of jasper, of the harps of gold, of the songs of bliss, and then her eyes glistened; she said, "Yes, I shall be there soon; I shall see them by-and-by;" and then she seemed so glad.

Ah, believer, you may always cheer yourself with that thought! Thy head may be crowned with thorny troubles now, but it shall wear a starry crown presently; thy hand may be filled with cares, it shall grasp a harp soon, a harp full of music. Thy garments may be soiled with dust now; they shall be white by-and-by. Wait a little longer. Ah, beloved! how despicable our troubles and trials will seem when we look back upon them! Looking at them here in the prospect, they seem immense; but when we get to heaven, they will seem to us just nothing at all; we shall talk to one another about them in heaven, and find all the more to converse about, according as we have suffered more here below. Let us go on, therefore; and if the night be ever so dark, remember there is not a night that shall not have a morning; and that morning is to come by-and-by. When sinners are lost in darkness, *we* shall lift up our eyes in everlasting light. Surely I need not dwell longer on this thought. There is matter enough for songs in the night in the past, the present, and the future.

## The Excellences of Our Songs in the Night

III. And now I want to tell you, very briefly, WHAT ARE THE EXCELLENCES OF SONGS IN THE NIGHT ABOVE ALL OTHER SONGS.

In the first place, when you hear a man singing a song in the night,—I mean in the night of trouble,—you may be quite sure it is *a hearty one*. Many of you sing very heartily now; I wonder whether you would sing as loudly if there were a stake or two in Smithfield for all of you who dared to do it. If you sang under pain and penalty, that would show your heart to be in your song. We can all sing very nicely indeed when everybody else sings; it is the easiest thing in the world to open our mouth, and let the words come out; but when the devil puts his hand over our mouth, can we sing then? Can you say, "Though he slay me, yet will I trust in him"? That is hearty singing, that is real song that springs up in the night.

Again, the song we sing in the night will be *lasting*. Many songs we hear our fellow-creatures singing will not do to sing by-and-by. They can sing now rollicking drinking songs; but they will not sing them when they come to die. No; but the Christian who can sing in the night, will not have to leave off his song; he may keep on singing it for ever. He may put his foot in Jordan's stream, and continue his melody; he may wade through it, and keep on singing still until he is landed safe in heaven; and when he is there, there need not be a pause in his strain, but in a nobler, sweeter song he may still continue singing the Savior's power to save.

Again, the songs we warble in the night are those that show we have *real faith in God*. Many men have just enough faith to trust God as far as providence goes as they think right; but true faith can sing when its possessors cannot see, it can take hold of God when they cannot discern him.

Songs in the night, too, prove that we have *true courage*. Many sing by day who are silent by night, they are afraid of thieves and robbers; but the Christian who sings in the night proves himself to be a courageous character. It is the bold Christian who can sing God's sonnets in the darkness.

He who can sing songs in the night, proves also that he has *true love to Christ*. It is not love to Christ merely to praise him while everybody else praises him; to walk arm in arm with him when he has the crown on his head, is no great thing to do. To walk with Christ in rags, is something more. To believe in Christ when he is shrouded in darkness, to stick hard and fast by the Savior when all men speak ill of him, and forsake him,—that proves true faith and love. He who singeth a song to Christ in the night, singeth the best song in all the world, for he singeth from the heart.

## The Use of Our Songs in the Night

IV. I will not dwell further on the excellences of night songs, but just, in the last place, SHOW YOU THEIR USE.

Well, beloved, it is very useful to sing in the night of our troubles, first, *because it will cheer ourselves*. When some of you were boys, living in the country, and had some distance to go alone at night, do you not remember how you whistled and sang to keep your courage up? Well, what we do in the natural world, we ought to do in the spiritual. There is nothing like singing to keep up our spirits. When we have been in trouble, we have often thought ourselves to be well-nigh overwhelmed with difficulty; so we have said, "Let us have a song." We have begun to sing; and we have proved the truth of what Martin Luther says, "The devil cannot bear singing, he does not like music."

It was so in Saul's day; an evil spirit rested on him, but when David played his harp, the evil spirit went from him. This is usually the case; and if we can begin to sing, we shall remove our fears. I like to hear servants sometimes humming a tune at their work; I love to hear a ploughman in the country singing as he goes along with his horses. Why not? You say he has no time to praise

God; but if he can sing a song, surely he can sing a psalm, it will take no more time. Singing is the best thing to purge ourselves of evil thoughts. Keep your mouth full of songs, and you will often keep your heart full of praises; keep on singing as long as you can, you will find it a good method of driving away your fears.

Sing in trouble, again, *because God loves to hear his people sing in the night*. At no time does God love his children's singing so well as when he has hidden his face from them, and they are all in darkness. "Ah!" says God, "that is true faith that can make them sing praises when I do not appear to them; I know there is faith in them, that makes them lift up their hearts, even when I seem to withhold from them all my tender mercies and all my compassions." Sing then, Christian, for singing pleases God. In heaven we read that the angels are employed in singing, be you employed in the same way; for by no better means can you gratify the Almighty One of Israel, who stoops from his high throne to observe us poor, feeble creatures of a day.

Sing, again, for another reason; *because it will cheer your companions*. If any of them are in the valley and in the darkness with you, it will be a great help to comfort them. John Bunyan tells us that, as Christian was going through the valley, he found it a dreadful place; horrible demons and hobgoblins were all about him, and poor Christian thought he must perish for certain; but just when his doubts were the strongest, he heard a sweet voice; he listened to it, and he heard a man in front of him singing, "Yea, though I walk through the valley of the shadow of death, I will fear no evil." Now, that man did not know who was near him, but he was unwittingly cheering a pilgrim behind.

Christian, when you are in trouble, sing; you do not

know who is near you. Sing! perhaps you will get a good companion by it. Sing! perhaps there will be another heart cheered by your song. There is some broken spirit, it may be, that will be bound up by your sonnets. Sing! there is some poor distressed brother, perhaps, shut up in the Castle of Despair, who, like King Richard, will hear your song inside the walls, and sing to you again, and you may be the means of getting him ransomed and released. Sing, Christian, wherever you go; try, if you can, to wash your face every morning in a bath of praise. When you go down from your chamber, never go to look on man till you have first looked on your God; and when you have looked on him, seek to come down with a face beaming with joy,—carry a smile, for you will cheer up many a poor, wayworn pilgrim by it. And when thou fastest, Christian, when thou hast an aching heart, do not appear to men to fast, appear cheerful and happy; anoint thy head, and wash thy face; be happy for thy brother's sake; it will tend to cheer him up, and help him through the valley.

One more reason, and I know it will be a good one for you. Try and sing in the night, Christian, *for that is one of the best arguments in all the world in favor of your religion.* Our divines nowadays spend a great deal of time in trying to prove the truth of Christianity to those who disbelieve it; I should like to have seen Paul trying that plan. Elymas the sorcerer withstood him; how did Paul treat him? He said, "O full of all subtlety and all mischief, thou child of the devil, thou enemy of all righteousness, wilt thou not cease to pervert the right ways of the Lord?" That is about all the politeness such men ought to have when they deny God's truth; we start with this assumption, that the Bible is God's Word, but we are not going to prove God's Word. If you do not believe it, we will bid you "Good-bye;" we will not argue with you. Religion is not a thing merely for your intellect to prove the greatness of your own talent; it is a thing that demands your faith. As a messenger of heaven, I demand that faith; if you do not choose to give it, on your own head be your doom.

O Christian, instead of disputing, let me tell you how to prove your religion! Live it out! Live it out! Give the external as well as the internal evidence; give the external evidence of your own life. You are sick; there is your neighbor, who laughs at religion, let him come into your house. When he was sick, he said, "Oh! send for the doctor;" and there he was fretting, and fuming, and making all manner of noises. When you are sick, send for him; tell him that you are resigned to the Lord's will, that you will kiss the chastening rod, that you will take the cup, and drink it, because your Father gives it. You need not make a boast of this, or it will lose all its power: but do it because you cannot help doing it. Your neighbor will say, "There is something in such a religion as that."

And when you come to the borders of the grave (he was there once, and you heard how he shrieked, and how frightened he was), give him your hand, and say to him, "Ah! I have a Christ who is with me now, I have a religion that will make me sing in the night." Let him hear how you can sing, "Victory, victory, victory," through him that loved you. I tell you, we may preach fifty thousand sermons to prove the gospel, but we shall not prove it half so well as you will through singing in the night. Keep a cheerful face, keep a happy heart, keep a contented spirit, keep your eye bright, and your heart aloft, and you will prove Christianity better than all the Butlers, and all the wise men who ever lived. Give them the "analogy" of a holy life, and then you will prove religion to them; give them the "evidences" of internal piety, developed externally, and you will give the best possible proof of Christianity. Try and sing songs in the night; for they are so rare that, if thou canst sing them, thou wilt honor thy God, and bless thy friends.

I have been all this while addressing the children of God, and now there is a sad turn that this subject must take; just a word or so, and then I have done. There is a night coming, in which there will be no songs of joy,—a night when a song shall be sung, of which misery shall be the subject, set to the music of wailing and gnashing of teeth; there is a night coming when woe, unutterable woe, shall be the theme of an awful, terrific *miserere*. There is a night coming for the poor soul, and unless he repent, it will be a night wherein he will have to sigh, and cry, and moan, and groan for ever.

I hope I shall never preach a sermon without speaking to the ungodly, for oh, how I love them! Swearer, your mouth is black with oaths now; and if you die, you must go on blaspheming throughout eternity, and be punished for it throughout eternity! But list to me, blasphemer! Dost thou repent? Dost thou feel thyself to have sinned against God? Dost thou feel a desire to be saved? List thee! thou mayest be saved; thou mayest be saved. There is another; she has sinned against God enormously, and she blushes even now while I mention her case; dost thou repent of thy sin? Then there is pardon for thee; remember him who said, "Go, and sin no more." Drunkard! but a little while ago thou wast reeling down the street, and now thou repentest; drunkard, there is hope for thee.

"Well," sayest thou, "what shall I do to be saved?" Let me again tell thee the old way of salvation; it is, "Believe on the Lord Jesus Christ, and thou shalt be saved." We can get no further than that, do what we will; this is the sum and substance of the gospel. "He that believeth and is baptized shall be saved." So saith the Savior himself. Dost thou ask, "What is it to believe?" Am I to tell thee again? I cannot tell thee except that it is to look to Christ. Dost thou see the Savior there? He is hanging on the cross; there are his dear hands, pierced with nails, fastened to a tree, as if they were waiting for thy tardy footsteps, because thou wouldst not come. Dost thou see his dear head there? It is hanging on his breast, as if he would lean over, and kiss thy poor soul. Dost thou see his blood, gushing from his head, his hands, his feet, his side? It is running after thee, because he well knew that thou wouldst never run after him.

Sinner, to be saved, all thou hast to do is to look at that Man! Canst thou not do it now? "No," thou sayest, "I do not believe that will save me." Ah, my poor friend, try it, I beseech thee, try it; and if thou dost not succeed, when thou hast tried it, I will be bondsman for my Lord,—here, take me, bind me, and I will suffer thy doom for thee. This I will venture to say; if thou castest thyself on Christ, and he deserteth thee, I will be willing to go halves with thee in all thy misery and woe; for he will never do it, never, *never*, NEVER!

> No sinner was ever empty sent back,
> Who came seeking mercy for Jesus's sake.

I beseech thee, therefore, try him, and thou shalt not try him in vain; but thou shalt find him "able to save them to the uttermost that come unto God by him;" and thou shalt be saved now, and saved for ever.

*"Everybody's Sermon,"* delivered July 25, 1858, is another one of Spurgeon's sermons that is often reprinted. Spurgeon is at his best here in his use of illustrations taken from every-day life. What he presents is a vision of earth in which everything in our lives—every time and every place, every animal and every kind of scenery, and especially every vocation—contains a sermon for men, if they are willing to listen. Spurgeon's title is appropriate, for he shows how God speaks to all men in their daily lives, whether they are farmers or butchers, physicians or jewellers.

## CHAPTER FIVE

# *Everybody's Sermon*

*I have multiplied visions, and used similitudes (Hos. 12:10).*

When the Lord would win his people Israel from their iniquities, he did not leave a stone unturned, but gave them precept upon precept, line upon line, here a little and there a little. He taught them sometimes with a rod in his hand, when he smote them with sore famine and pestilence, and invasion; at other times he sought to win them with bounties, for he multiplied their corn and their wine and their oil, and he laid no famine upon them. But all the teachings of his providence were unavailing, and whilst his hand was stretched out, still they continued to rebel against the Most High. He hewed them by the prophets. He sent them first one, and then another; the golden-mouthed Isaiah was followed by the plaintive Jeremy; while at his heels, in quick succession, there followed many far-seeing, thunder-speaking seers. But though prophet followed prophet in quick succession, each of them uttering the burning words of the Most High, yet they would have none of his rebukes, but they hardened their hearts, and went on still in their iniquities.

Among the rest of God's agencies for striking their attention and their conscience, was the use of similitudes. The prophets were accustomed not only to preach, but to be themselves as signs and wonders to the people. For instance, Isaiah named his child, Maher-shalal-hash-baz, that they might know that the judgment of the Lord was hastening upon them; and this child was ordained to be a sign, "for before the child shall have knowledge to cry, my father and my mother, the riches of Damascus and the spoil of Samaria shall be taken away before the king of Assyria." On another occasion, the Lord said unto Isaiah, "Go and loose the sackcloth from off thy loins, and put off thy shoe from thy foot." And he did so, walking naked and barefoot. And the Lord said, "Like as my servant Isaiah hath walked naked and barefoot three years for a sign and wonder upon Egypt and upon Ethiopia; so shall the king of Assyria lead away the Egyptians prisoners, and the Ethiopians captives young and old, naked and barefoot, to the shame of Egypt."

Hosea, the prophet, himself had to teach the people by a similitude. You will notice in the first chapter a most extraordinary similitude. The Lord said to him, "Go, take unto thee a wife of whoredoms; for the land hath committed great whoredom, departing from the Lord;" and he did so, and the children begotten by this marriage were made as signs and wonders to the people. As for his first son, he was to be called Jezreel, "for yet a little while, and I will avenge the blood of Jezreel upon the house of Jehu." As for his daughter, she was to be called Lo-ruhamah, "for I will no more have mercy upon the house of Israel; but I will utterly take them away." Thus by divers significant signs, God made the people think.

He made his prophets do strange things, in order that the people might talk about what he had done, and then the meaning which God would have them learn, should come home more powerfully to their consciences, and be the better remembered.

God is every day preaching to us by similitudes. When Christ was on earth he preached in parables, and, though he is in heaven now, he is preaching in parables to-day. Providence is God's sermon. The things which we see about us are God's thoughts and God's words to us; and if we were but wise there is not a step that we take, which we should not find to be full of mighty instruction. O ye sons of men! God warns you every day by his own word; he speaks to you by the lips of his servants, his ministers; but, besides this, by similitudes he addresses you at every time. He leaves no stone unturned to bring his wandering children to himself, to make the lost sheep of the house of Israel return to the fold. In addressing myself to you this morning, I shall endeavor to show how every day, and every season of the year, in every place, and in every calling which you are made to exercise, God is speaking to you by similitudes.

## Similitudes in Daily Life

I. EVERY DAY God speaks to you by similitudes. Let us begin with the *early morning*. This morning you awakened and you found yourselves unclothed, and you began to array yourselves in your garments. Did not God, if you would but have heard him, speak to you by a similitude? Did he not as much as say to thee, "Sinner, what will it be when thy vain dreams shall have ended, if thou shouldst wake up in eternity to find thyself naked? Wherewithal shalt thou array thyself? If in this life thou

dost cast away the wedding garment, the spotless righteousness of Jesus Christ, what wilt thou do when the
trump of the archangel shall awaken thee from thy clay
cold couch in the grave, when the heavens shall be blaz-
ing with lightnings, and the solid pillars of the earth
shall quake with the terrors of God's thunder? How wilt
thou be able to dress thyself then?" Canst thou confront
thy Maker without a covering for thy nakedness? Adam
dared not, and canst thou attempt it? Will he not affright
thee with his terrors? Will he not cast thee to the tormen-
tors that thou mayest be burned with unquenchable fire,
because thou didst forget the clothing of thy soul while
thou wast in this place of probation?

Well, you have put on your dress, and you come down
to your families, and your children gather round your
table for the morning meal. If you have been wise, *God
has been preaching to you by a similitude then:* he seemed
to say to thee—"Sinner, to whom should a child go but to
his father? And where should be his resort when he is
hungry but to his father's table?" And as you fed your
children, if you had an ear to hear, the Lord was speaking to you and saying. "How willingly would I feed you!
How would I give you of the bread of heaven and cause
you to eat angels' food! But thou hast spent thy money
for that which is not bread, and thy labor for that which
satisfieth not. Hearken diligently unto me, and eat ye
that which is good, let thy soul delight itself in fatness."
Did he not stand there as a Father, and say, "Come, my
child, come to my table. The precious blood of my Son
has been shed to be thy drink, and he has given his body
to be thy bread. Why wilt thou wander hungry and
thirsty? Come to my table, O my child, for I love my children to be there and to feast upon the mercies I have provided."

You left your home and you went to your business. I know not in what calling your time was occupied—of that we will say more before we shall have gathered up the ends of your similitudes this morning—but you spend your time in your work; and surely, beloved, all the time that your fingers were occupied, God was speaking to your heart if the ears of your soul had not been closed, so that you were heavy and ready to slumber, and could not hear his voice. And when the sun was shining in high heaven, and the hour of noon was reached, mightest thou not have lifted up thine eye and remembered that if thou hadst committed thy soul to God, thy path should have been as the shining light which shineth more and more unto the perfect day? Did he not speak to thee and say, "I brought the sun from the darkness of the east; I have guided him and helped him to ascend the slippery steeps of heaven, and now he standeth in his zenith, like a giant that hath run his race, and hath attained his goal. And even so will I do with thee. Commit thy ways unto me and I will make thee full of light, and thy path shall be as brightness, and thy life shall be as the noon-day; thy sun shall not go down by day, but the days of thy morning shall be ended, for the Lord God shall be thy light and thy salvation."

And the sun began to set, and the shadows of evening were drawing on, and did not the Lord then remind thee of thy death? Suns have their setting, and men have their graves. When the shadows of the evening were stretched out, and when the darkness began to gather, did he not say unto thee, "O, man, take heed of thine eventide, for the light of the sun shall not endure for ever? There are twelve hours wherein a man shall work, but when they are past there is no work nor device in the night of that grave whither we are all hastening. Work while ye have the light, for the night cometh wherein no man can work. Therefore, whatsoever thine hand findeth to do, do it with all thy might."

Look, I say, to the sun at his setting, and observe the rainbow hues of glory with which he paints the sky, and mark how he appears to increase his orb, as he nears the horizon. O man, kneel down and learn this prayer—"Lord, let my dying be like the setting of the sun; help me, if clouds and darkness are round about me, to light them up with splendor; surround me, O my God, with a greater brightness at my death than I have shown in all my former life. If my death-bed shall be the miserable pallet, and if I expire in some lone cot, yet nevertheless, grant, O Lord, that my poverty may be gilded with the light that thou shalt give me, and that I may exhibit the grandeur of a Christian's departure at my dying hour." God speaketh to thee, O man, by similitude, from the rising to the setting of the sun.

And now, thou hast lit thy candles and thou sittest down; thy children are about thee, and the Lord sends thee a little preacher to preach thee a sermon, if thou wilt hear. It is a little gnat, and it flieth round and round about thy candle, and delighteth itself in the light thereof, till, dazzled and intoxicated, it begins to singe its wings and burn itself. Thou seekest to put it away, but it dashes into the flame, and having burned itself it can scarcely fan itself through the air again. But as soon as it has recruited its strength again, mad-like it dashes to its death and destruction.

Did not the Lord say to thee, "Sinner, thou art doing this also; thou lovest the light of sin; oh, that thou wert wise enough to tremble at the fire of sin, for he who delights in the sparks thereof must be consumed in the burning"? Did not thy hand seem to be like the hand of the Almighty, who would put thee away from thine own destruction, and who rebukes and smites thee by his providence, as much as to say to thee, "Poor silly man, be not thine own destruction"? And while thou seest perhaps with a little sorrow the death of the foolish insect, might not that forewarn thee of thine awful doom, when, after having been dazzled with the giddy round of this world's joys, thou shalt at last plunge into the eternal burning and lose thy soul, so madly, for nothing but the enjoyments of an hour? Doth not God preach to thee thus?

And now it is time for thee to retire to thy rest. Thy door is bolted, and thou hast fast closed it. Did not that remind thee of that saying, "When once the master of the house is risen up, and hath shut to the door, and ye begin to stand without, and to knock at the door, saying, 'Lord, Lord, open unto us;' and he shall answer and say unto you, 'I know not whence you are'"? In vain shall be your knocking then, when the bars of immutable justice shall have fast closed the gates of mercy on mankind; when the hand of the Almighty Master shall have shut his children within the gates of paradise, and shall have left the thief and the robber in the cold chilly darkness, the outer darkness, where there shall be weeping and wailing and gnashing of teeth. Did he not preach to thee by similitude? Even then, when thy finger was on the bolt, might not his finger have been on thy heart?

And at night time thou wast startled. The watchman in the street awoke thee with the cry of the hour of the night, or his tramp along the street. O man, if thou hadst ears to hear, thou mightest have heard in the steady tramp of the policeman the cry, "Behold, the bridegroom cometh; go ye out to meet him." And every sound at midnight that did awaken thee from thy slumber and startle thee upon thy bed, might seem to forewarn thee of that dread trump of the archangel which shall herald the coming of the Son of man, in the day he shall judge both the quick and the dead, according to my gospel. O that ye were wise, that ye understood this, for all the day long from dewy morning till the darkness of the eventide, and the thick darkness of midnight, God evermore doth preach to man—he preacheth to him by similitudes.

## Similitudes Throughout the Year

II.  And now we turn the current of our thoughts, and observe that ALL THE YEAR round God doth preach to man by similitudes. It was but a little while ago that we were sowing our seeds in our garden, and scattering the corn over the broad furrows. God had sent the seed time, to remind us that we too are like the ground, and that he is scattering seed in our hearts each day. And did he not say to us, "Take heed, O man, lest thou shouldst be like the highway whereon the seed was scattered, but the fowls of the air devoured it. Take heed that thou be not like the ground that had its basement on a hard and arid rock, lest this seed should spring up and by-and-by should wither away when the sun arose, because it had not much depth of earth. And be thou careful, O son of man, that thou art not like the ground where the seed did spring up, but the thorns sprang up and choked it; but be thou like the good ground whereon the seed did fall, and it brought forth fruit, some twenty, some fifty, and some a hundred fold."

We thought, when we were sowing the seed, that we expected one day to see it spring up again. Was there not a lesson for us there? Are not our actions all of them as seeds? Are not our little words like grains of mustard-seed? Is not our daily conversation like a handful of the corn that we scatter over the soil? And ought we not to remember that our words shall live again, that our acts are as immortal as ourselves, that after having laid a little while in the dust to be matured, they shall certainly arise? The black deeds of sin shall bear a dismal harvest of damnation; and the right deeds which God's grace has permitted us to do, shall, through his mercy and not through our merit, bring forth a bounteous harvest in the day when they who sow in tears shall reap in joy. Doth not seed time preach to thee, O man, and say, "Take heed that thou sowest good seed in thy field."

And when the seed sprang up, and the season had changed, did God cease then to preach? Ah! no. First the blade, then the ear, and then the full corn in the ear, had each its homily. And when at last the harvest came, how loud the sermon which it preached to us! It said to us, "O Israel, I have set a harvest for thee. Whatsoever a man soweth that shall he also reap. He that soweth to the flesh shall of the flesh reap corruption, and he that soweth to the Spirit shall of the Spirit reap life everlasting."

If you have to journey in the country, you will, if your heart is rightly attuned, find a marvelous mass of wisdom couched in a corn-field. Why, I could not attempt for a moment to open the mighty mines of golden treasure which are hidden there. Think, beloved, of the joy of the harvest. How does it tell us of the joy of the redeemed, if we, being saved, shall at last be carried like shocks of corn fully ripe into the garner. Look at the ear of corn when it is fully ripe, and see how it dippeth toward the earth! It held its head erect before, but in getting ripe how humble does it become! And how does God speak to the sinner, and tell him, that if he would be fit for the great harvest he must drop his head and cry, "Lord have mercy upon me a sinner." And when we see the weeds spring up amongst wheat, have we not our Master's parable over again of the tares among the wheat; and are we not reminded of the great day of division, when he shall say to the reaper, "Gather first the tares and bind them in bundles, to burn them; but gather the wheat into my barn."

O yellow field of corn, thou preachest well to me, for thou sayest to me, the minister, "Behold, the fields are ripe already to the harvest. Work thou thyself, and pray thou the Lord of the harvest to send forth more laborers into the harvest." And it preaches well to thee, thou man of years, it tells thee that the sickle of death is sharp, and that thou must soon fall, but it cheers and comforts thee, for it tells thee that the wheat shall be safely housed, and it bids thee hope that thou shalt be carried to thy Master's garner to be his joy and his delight for ever. Hark, then, to the rustling eloquence of the yellow harvest.

In a very little time, my beloved, you will see the birds congregated on the housetops in great multitudes, and after they have whirled round and round and round, as if they were taking their last sight at Old England, or rehearsing their supplications before they launched away, you will see them, with their leader in advance, speed across the purple sea to live in sunnier climes, while winter's cold hand shall strip their native woods. And doth not God seem to preach to you, sinners, when these birds are taking their flight? Do you not remember how he himself puts it? "Yea, the stork in the heaven knoweth her appointed times; and the turtle, and the crane, and the swallow, observe the time of their coming; but my people know not the judgment of the Lord." Doth he not tell us that there is a time of dark winter coming upon this world; a time of trouble, such as there has been none like it, neither shall be any more; a time, when all the joys of sin shall be nipped and frost-bitten, and when the summer of man's estate shall be turned into the dark winter of his disappointment? And does he not say to you, "Sinner! fly away—away—away to the goodly land, where Jesus dwells! Away from self and sin! Away from the city of destruction! Away from the whirl of pleasures, and from the tossing to and fro of trouble! Haste thee, like a bird to its rest! Fly thou across the sea of repentance and faith, and build thy nest in the land of mercy, that when the great day of vengeance shall pass o'er this world, thou mayest be safe in the clefts of the rock."

I remember well, how once God preached to me by a similitude in the depth of winter. The earth had been black, and there was scarcely a green thing or a flower to be seen. As you looked across the field, there was nothing but blackness—bare hedges and leafless trees, and black, black earth, wherever you looked. On a sudden God spake, and unlocked the treasures of the snow, and white flakes descended until there was no blackness to be seen, and all was one sheet of dazzling whiteness. It was at that time that I was seeking the Savior, and it was then I found him; and I remember well that sermon which I saw before me; "Come now, and let us reason together; though your sins be as scarlet they shall be as snow, though they be red like crimson they shall be whiter than wool."

Sinner! thy heart is like that black ground; thy soul is like that black tree and hedgerow, without leaf or blossom; God's grace is like the white snow—it shall fall upon thee till thy doubting heart shall glitter in whiteness of pardon, and thy poor black soul shall be covered with the spotless purity of the Son of God. He seems to say to you, "Sinner, you are black, but I am ready to forgive you; I will wrap thy heart in the ermine of my Son's righteousness, and with my Son's own garments on, thou shalt be holy as the Holy One."

And the *wind* of to-day, as it comes howling through the trees—many of which have been swept down—reminds us of the Spirit of the Lord, which "bloweth where it listeth," and when it pleaseth; and it tells us to seek earnestly after that divine and mysterious influence which alone can speed us on our voyage to heaven; which shall cast down the trees of our pride, and tear up by the roots the goodly cedars of our self-confidence; which shall shake our refuges of lies about our ears, and make us look to him who is the only covert from the storm, the only shelter when "the blast of the terrible ones is as a storm against the wall."

Ay, and when the *heat* is coming down, and we hide ourselves beneath the shadow of the tree, an angel standeth there, and whispereth, "Look upwards, sinner, as thou hidest thyself from the burning rays of Sol beneath the tree; so there is One who is like the apple tree among the trees of the wood, and he bids thee come and take shadow beneath his branches, for he will screen thee from the eternal vengeance of God, and give thee shelter when the fierce heat of God's anger shall beat upon the heads of wicked men."

## Similitudes in Every Place

III. And now again, EVERY PLACE to which you journey, every *animal* that you see, every *spot* you visit, has a sermon for you. Go into your farm-yard, and your ox and your ass shall preach to you. "The ox knoweth his owner, and the ass his master's crib; but Israel doth not know, my people doth not consider." The very dog at your heels may rebuke you. He follows his master; a stranger will he not follow, for he knows not the voice of a stranger, but ye forsake your God and turn aside unto your crooked ways. Look at the chicken by the side of yonder pond, and let it rebuke your ingratitude. It drinks, and every sip it takes it lifts its head to heaven and thanks the Giver of the rain for the drink afforded to it; while thou eatest and drinkest, and there is no blessing pronounced at thy meals, and no thanksgiving bestowed upon thy Father for his bounty. The very horse is checked by the bridle, and the whip is for the ass; but thy God hath bridled thee by his commandments, and he hath chastened by his providence, yet art thou more obstinate than the ass or the mule; still thou wilt not run in his commandments, but thou turnest aside, willfully and wickedly following out the perversity of thine own heart.

Is it not so? Are not these things true of you? If you are still without God and without Christ, must not these things strike your conscience? Would not any one of them lead you to tremble before the Most High, and beg of him that he would give you a new heart and a right spirit, and that no longer you might be as the beasts of the field, but might be a man of the divine Spirit, living in obedience to your Creator.

And in *journeying*, you have noticed how often the road is rough with stones, and you have murmured because of the way over which you have to tread; and have you not thought that those stones were helping to make the road better, and that the worst piece of road when mended with hard stones would in time become smooth and fit to travel on? And did you think how often God has mended you; how many stones of affliction he has cast upon you;

how many wagon loads of warnings you have had spread out upon you, and you have been none the better, but have only grown worse; and when he comes to look on you to see whether your life has become smooth, whether the highway of your moral conduct has become more like the king's highway of righteousness, how might he say, "Alas! I have repaired this road, but it is none the better; let it alone until it becomes a very bog and quagmire, until he who keeps it thus ill shall have perished in it himself."

And thou hast gone by the sea-side, and has not the sea talked to thee? Inconstant as the sea art thou, but thou art not one half so obedient. God keeps the sea, the mountain-waved sea, in check with a belt of sand; he spreads the sand along the sea-shore, and even the sea observes the landmark. "Fear ye not me? saith the Lord; will ye not tremble at my presence, which have placed the sand for the bound of the sea by a perpetual decree, that it can not pass it; and though the waves thereof toss themselves, yet can they not prevail; though they roar, yet can they not pass over it?" It is so. Let thy conscience prick thee. The sea obeys him from shore to shore, and yet thou wilt not have him to be thy God, but thou sayest, "Who is the Lord that I should fear him? Who is Jehovah that I should acknowledge his sway?"

Hear the *mountains* and the *hills*, for they have a lesson. Such is God. He abideth for ever—think not that he shall change.

And now, sinner, I entreat thee to open thine eyes as thou goest home to-day, and if nothing that I have said shall smite thee, perhaps God shall put into thy way something that shall give thee a text, from which thou mayest preach to thyself a sermon that never shall be forgotten. Oh! if I had but time, and thought, and words,

I would bring the things that are in heaven above, and in the earth beneath, and in the waters under the earth, and I would set them all before thee, and they should every one give their warning before they had passed from thine inspection, and I know that their voice would be, "Consider the Lord, thy Creator, and fear and serve him, for he hath made thee, and thou hast not made thyself;" we obey him, and we find it is our beauty to be obedient, and our glory ever to move according to his will; and thou shalt find it to be the same.

Obey him while thou mayest, lest haply when this life is over all these things shall rise up against thee, and the stone in the street shall clamor for thy condemnation, and the beam out of the wall shall bear witness against thee, and the beasts of the field shall be thine accusers, and the valley and hill shall begin to curse thee. O man, the earth is made for thy warning. God would have thee be saved. He hath set hand posts everywhere in nature and in providence, pointing thee the way to the city of refuge, and if thou art but wise thou needest not miss thy way; it is but thy willful ignorance and thy neglect that shall cause thee to run on in the way of error, for God hath made the way straight before thee and given thee every encouragement to run therein.

## Similitudes in Every Calling

IV.  And now, lest I should weary you, I will just notice that every man in his CALLING has a sermon preached to him.

The *farmer* has a thousand sermons; I have brought them out already; let him open wide his eyes, and he shall see more. He need not go an inch without hearing the songs of angels, and the voices of spirits wooing him to righteousness, for all nature round about him has a tongue given to it, when man hath an ear to hear.

There are others, however, engaged in a business which allows them to see but very little of nature, and yet even there God has provided them with a lesson. There is the *baker* who provides us with our bread. He thrusts his fuel into the oven, and he causeth it to glow with heat, and he puts bread therein. Well may he, if he be an ungodly man, tremble as he stands at the oven's mouth, for there is a text which he may well comprehend as he stands there: "For the day cometh that shall burn as an oven, and all the proud and they that do wickedly shall be as stubble; they shall be consumed. Men ingather them in bundles and cast them into the fire, and they are burned." Out of the oven's mouth comes a hot and burning warning, and the man's heart might melt like wax within him if he would but regard it.

Then see the *butcher*. How doth the beast speak to him? He sees the lamb almost lick his knife, and the bullock goes unconsciously to the slaughter. How might he think every time that he smites the unconscious animal (who knows nothing of death), of his own doom. Are we not, all of us who are without Christ, fattening for the slaughter? Are we not more foolish than the bullock, for doth not the wicked man follow his executioner, and walk after his own destroyer into the very chambers of hell? When we see a drunkard pursuing his drunkenness, or an unchaste man running in the way of licentiousness, is he not as an ox going to the slaughter, until a dart smite him through the liver? Hath not God sharpened his knife and made ready his ax that the fatlings of this earth may be killed, when he shall say to the fowls of the air and the beasts of the field, "Behold, I have made a feast of vengeance for you, and ye shall feast upon the blood of the slain, and make yourselves drunken with the streams thereof"? Ay, butcher, there is a lecture for you in your trade; and your business may reproach you.

And ye whose craft is to sit still all day, making shoes for our feet, the lapstone in your lap may reproach you, for your heart, perhaps, is as hard as that. Have you not been smitten as often as your lapstone, and yet your heart has never been broken or melted? And what shall the Lord say to you at last, when your stony heart being still within you, he shall condemn you and cast you away because you would have none of his rebukes and would not turn at the voice of his exhortation.

Let the *brewer* remember that as he brews he must drink. Let the *potter* tremble lest he be like a vessel marred upon the wheel. Let the *printer* take heed, that his life be set in heavenly type, and not in the black letter of sin. *Painter,* beware! for paint will not suffice, we must have unvarnished realities.

Others of you are engaged in business where you are continually using scales and measures. Might you not often put yourselves into those scales? Might you not fancy you saw the great Judge standing by with his gospel in one scale and you in the other, and solemnly looking down upon you, saying, "*Mene, mene, tekel*—thou art weighed in the balances and found wanting"? Some of you use the measure, and when you have measured out, you cut off the portion that your customer requires. Think of your life too, it is to be of a certain length, and every year brings the measure a little further, and at last there come the scissors that shall clip off your life, and it is done. How knowest thou when thou art come to the last inch? What is that disease thou hast about thee, but the first snip of the scissors? What that trembling in thy bones, that failing in thy eyesight, that fleeing of thy memory, that departure of thy youthful vigor, but the first rent? How soon shalt thou be rent in twain, the remnant of thy days past away, and thy years all numbered and gone, misspent and wasted for ever!

But you say you are engaged as a *servant* and your occupations are diverse. Then diverse are the lectures God preaches to you. "A servant waits for his wages and the hireling fulfilleth his day." There is a similitude for thee, when thou hast fulfilled thy day on earth, and shalt take thy wages at last. Who then is thy master? Art thou serving Satan and the lusts of the flesh, and wilt thou take out thy wages at last in the hot metal of destruction? or art thou serving the fair prince Emmanuel, and shalt thy wages be the golden crowns of heaven? Oh! happy art thou if thou servest a good master, for according to thy master shall be thy reward; as is thy labor such shall the end be.

Or art thou one that *guideth the pen*, and from hour to hour wearily thou writest? Ah! man, know that thy life is a writing. When thy hand is not on the pen, thou art a writer still; thou art always writing upon the pages of eternity; thy sins thou art writing or else thy holy confidence in him that loved thee. Happy shall it be for thee, O writer, if thy name is written in the Lamb's book of life, and if that black writing of thine, in the history of thy pilgrimage below, shall have been blotted out with the red blood of Christ, and thou shalt have written upon thee, the fair name of Jehovah, to stand legible for ever.

Or perhaps thou art a *physician* or a *chemist;* thou prescribest or preparest medicines for man's body. God stands there by the side of thy pestle and thy mortar; and by the table where thou writest thy prescriptions, and he says to thee, "Man, thou art sick; I can prescribe for thee. The blood and righteousness of Christ, laid hold of by faith, and applied by the Spirit, can cure thy soul. I can compound a medicine for thee that shall rid thee of thy ills and bring thee to the place where the inhabitants shall no more say, 'I am sick.' Wilt thou take my medicine or wilt thou reject it? Is it bitter to thee, and dost thou turn away from it? Come, drink my child, drink, for thy life lieth here; and how shalt thou escape if thou neglect so great salvation?" Do you cast iron, or melt lead, or fuse the hard metals of the mines? then pray that the Lord may melt thine heart and cast thee in the mold of the gospel! Do you make garments for men? oh, be careful that you find a garment for yourself for ever.

Are you busy in *building* all day long, laying the stone upon its fellow and the mortar in its crevice? Then remember thou art building for eternity too. Oh that thou mayest thyself be built upon a good foundation! Oh that thou mayest build thereon, not wood, hay, or stubble, but gold, and silver, and precious stones, and things that will abide the fire! Take care, man, lest thou shouldest be God's scaffold, lest thou shouldest be used on earth to be a scaffolding for building his church, and when his church is built thou shouldest be cast down and burned up with fire unquenchable. Take heed that thou art built upon a rock, and not upon the sand, and that the vermilion cement of the Savior's precious blood unites thee to the foundation of the building, and to every stone thereof.

Art thou a *jeweler*, and dost thou cut the gem and polish the diamond from day to day? Would to God thou wouldest take warning from the contrast which thou presentest to the stone on which thou dost exercise thy craft. Thou cuttest it, and it glitters the more thou dost cut it; but though thou hast been cut and ground, though thou hast had cholera and fever, and hast been at death's door many a day, thou art none the brighter, but the duller, for alas! thou art no diamond. Thou art but the pebble-stone of the brook, and in the day when God makes up his jewels he shall not enclose thee in the casket of his treasures; for thou art not one of the precious sons of Zion, comparable unto fine gold. But be thy situation what it may, be thy calling what it may, there is a continual sermon preached to thy conscience. I would that thou wouldest now from this time forth open both eye and ear, and see and hear the things that God would teach thee.

And now, dropping the similitude while the clock shall tick but a few times more, let us put the matter thus—Sinner, thou art as yet without God and without Christ; thou art liable to death every hour. Thou canst not tell but that thou mayest be in the flames of hell before the clock shall strike ONE today. Thou art to-day "condemned already," because thou believest not in the Son of God. And Jesus Christ saith to thee this day, "Oh, that thou wouldest consider thy latter end!" He cries to thee this morning, "How often would I have gathered thee as a hen gathereth her chickens under her wings, but ye would not."

I entreat you, consider your ways. If it be worth while to make your bed in hell, do it. If the pleasures of this world are worth being damned to all eternity for enjoying them, if heaven be a cheat and hell a delusion, go on with your sins. But, if there be hell for sinners and heaven for repenting ones, and if thou must dwell a whole eternity in one place or the other, without similitude, I put a plain question to thee—Art thou wise in living as thou dost, without thought—careless, and godless?

Wouldst thou ask now the way of salvation? It is simply this—"Believe on the Lord Jesus Christ and thou shalt be saved." He died; he rose again; thou art to believe him to be thine; thou art to believe that he is able to save unto the uttermost them that come unto God by him. But, more than that, believing that to be a fact, thou art to cast thy soul upon that fact and trust to him, sink or swim. Spirit of God! help us each to do this; and by similitude, or by providence, or by thy prophets, bring us each to thyself and save us eternally, and unto thee shall be the glory.

*Among Spurgeon's most interesting sermons were some that he delivered upon special occasions, such as "India's Ills and England's Sorrows," given on September 6, 1857. When a mutiny had occurred in India against Britain's rule, a service of national humiliation was planned, and Spurgeon was asked to speak. The day before the service he tested the acoustics of the Crystal Palace, which had not been built to house such a meeting, by repeating, "Behold the Lamb of God which taketh away the sin of the world." His words were heard by a man who had been working in the building and who came to Spurgeon several days later to tell him that the message of the verse had caused him to come to know Christ.*

*23,654 attending the service, undoubtedly the largest indoor congregation up until that time. Spurgeon called for national repentance and humiliation and reminded his countrymen that only righteousness could exalt a nation. Spurgeon also took the opportunity to condemn the nation for all of its sins and exhorted his countrymen to weep.*

# CHAPTER SIX

## *India's Ills and England's Sorrows*

*Oh that my head were waters, and mine eyes a fountain of tears, that I might weep day and night for the slain of the daughter of my people (Jer. 9:1).*

Sometimes tears are base things; the offspring of a cowardly spirit. Some men weep when they should knit their brows, and many a woman weepeth when she should resign herself to the will of God. Many of those briny drops are but an expression of child-like weakness. It were well if we could wipe such tears away, and face a frowning world with a constant countenance. But oft times tears are the index of strength. There are periods when they are the noblest things in the world. The tears of penitents are precious: a cup of them were worth a king's ransom. It is no sign of weakness when a man weeps for sin, it shows that he hath strength of mind; nay more, that he hath strength imparted by God, which enables him to forswear his lusts and overcome his passions, and to turn unto God with full purpose of heart.

And there are other tears, too, which are the evidences not of weakness, but of might—the tears of tender sympathy are the children of strong affection, and they are strong like their parents. He that loveth much, must weep much; much love and much sorrow must go together in this vale of tears. The unfeeling heart, the unloving spirit, may pass from earth's portal to its utmost bound almost without a sigh except for itself; but he that loveth, hath digged as many wells of tears as he has chosen objects of affection; for by as many as our friends are multiplied, by so many must our griefs be multiplied too, if we have love enough to share in their griefs and to bear their burden for them. The largest hearted man will miss many sorrows that the little man will feel, but he will have to endure many sorrows the poor narrow-minded spirit never knoweth.

It needs a mighty prophet like Jeremiah to weep as mightily as he. Jeremiah was not weak in his weeping; the strength of his mind and the strength of his love were the parents of his sorrow. "Oh that my head were waters, and mine eyes a fountain of tears, that I might weep day and night for the slain of the daughter of my people." This is no expression of weak sentimentalism; this is no utterance of mere whining pretence; it is the burst of a strong soul, strong in its affection, strong in its devotion, strong in its self-sacrifice. I would to God we knew how to weep like this; and if we might not weep so frequently as Jeremy, I wish that when we did weep, we did weep as well.

It would seem as if some men had been sent into this world for the very purpose of being the world's weepers. God's great house is thoroughly furnished with everything; everything that can express the thoughts and the emotions of the inhabitant, God hath made. I find in nature, plants to be everlasting weepers. There by the lonely brook, where the maiden cast away her life, the willow weeps for ever; and there in the grave yard where men lie slumbering till the trumpet of the archangel shall awaken them, stands the dull cypress, mourning in its somber garments.

Now as it is with nature, so it is with the race of man. Mankind have bravery and boldness; they must have their heroes to express their courage. Mankind have some love to their fellow-creatures; they must have their fine philanthropists to live out mankind's philanthropy. Men have their sorrows; they must have their weepers; they must have men of sorrows who have it for their avocation, and their business, to weep, from the cradle to the grave; to be ever weeping, not so much for themselves as for the woes of others.

It may be I have some such here; I shall be happy to enlist their sympathies; and truly if I have none of that race, I shall boldly appeal to the whole mass of you, and I will bring before you causes of great grief; and when I bid you by the love you bear to man, and to his God, to begin to weep; if you have tears, these hard times will compel you to shed them now. Come, let me show you wherefore I have taken this my text, and why I have uttered this mournful language; and if your hearts be not as stolid as stone, sure there should be some tears shed this morning. For if I be not foolish in my utterances and faint in my speech, you will go home to your chambers to weep there. "Oh that *my* head were waters and *mine* eyes a fountain of tears, that I might weep day and night for the slain of the daughter of my people."

## Weeping for Persons Actually Slain

I want your griefs this morning, first, *for persons actu-*

*ally slain*—"the slain of the daughter of our people;" and then I shall need your tears *for those morally slain,* "the slain of the daughter of our people."

I. To begin, then, with ACTUAL MURDER AND REAL BLOODSHED. My brethren, our hearts are sick nigh unto death with the terrible news brought us post after post, telegraph after telegraph; we have read many letters of the *Times,* day after day, until we have folded up that paper, and professed before God that we could read no more. Our spirits have been harrowed by the most fearful and unexpected cruelty. We, perhaps, may not have been personally interested in the bloodshed, so far as our own husbands, wives, brothers, and sisters have been concerned, but we have felt the tie of kindred very strongly when we have found our race so cruelly butchered in the land of the East.

It is for us to-day humbly to confess our crime. The government of India has been a cruel government; it has much for which to appear before the bar of God. Its tortures—if the best evidence is to be believed—have been of the most inhuman kind; God forgive the men who have committed such crimes in the British name. But those days are past. May God blot out the sin. We do not forget our own guilt; but an overwhelming sense of the guilt of others, who have with such cold-hearted cruelty tormented men and women, may well excuse us if we do not dilate upon the subject.

Alas! alas, for our brethren there! They have died; alas for them! They have been slain by the sword of treachery, and traitorously murdered by men who swore allegiance. Alas for them! But, O ye soldiers, we weep not for you. Even when ye were tortured, ye had not that high dishonor to bear to which the other sex has been obliged to submit. O England! weep for thy daughters with a bitter lamentation; let thine eyes run down with rivers of blood for them. Had they been crushed within the folds of the hideous boa, or had the fangs of the tiger been red with their blood, happy would their fate have been compared with the indignities they have endured! O Earth! thou hast beheld crimes which antiquity could not parallel; thou hast seen bestial lust gratified upon the purest and the best of mortals. God's fairest creatures stained; those loved ones, who could not brook the name of lust, given up to the embraces of incarnate devils!

Weep, Britain, weep; weep for thy sons and for thy daughters! If thou art cold-hearted now, if thou readest the tale of infamy now without a tear, thou art no mother to them! Sure thine heart must have failed thee, and thou hast become less loving than thine own lions, and less tender than beasts of prey, if thou dost not weep for the maiden and the wife! Brethren, I am not straining history; I am not endeavoring to be pathetic where there is no pathos. No; my subject of itself is all pathos; it is my poor way of speaking that doth spoil it. I have not to-day to act the orator's part, to garnish up that which was nothing before; I have not to magnify little griefs—rather I feel that all my utterances do but diminish the woe which every thoughtful man must feel. Oh, how have our hearts been harrowed, cut in pieces, molten in the fire! Agony hath seized upon us, and grief unutterable, when, day after day, our hopes have been disappointed, and we have heard that still the rebel rages in his fury, and still with despotic might doth as he pleaseth with the sons and daughters, the husbands and the wives of England.

Weep, Christians, weep! And ye ask me of what avail shall be your weeping. I have bidden you weep to-day, because the spirit of vengeance is gathering; Britain's wrath is stirred; a black cloud is hanging over the head of the mutinous Sepoys! Their fate shall be most dreadful, their doom most tremendous, when England shall smite the murderers, as justly she must. There must be a judicial punishment enacted upon these men, so terrible that the earth shall tremble, and both the ears of him that heareth it shall tingle!

I am inclined, if I can, to sprinkle some few cooling tears upon the fires of vengeance. No, no; we will not take vengeance upon ourselves. "Vengeance is mine; I will repay, saith the Lord." Let not Britain's soldiers push their enemies to destruction, through a spirit of vengeance, as men; let them do it as the appointed executioners of the sentence of our laws. According to the civil code of every country under heaven, these men are condemned to die. Not as soldiers should we war with them, but as malefactors we must execute the law upon them. They have committed treason against government, and for that crime alone the doom is death! But they are murderers, and rightly or wrongly, our law is, that the murderer must die the death. God must have this enormous sin punished; and though we would feel no vengeance as Britons, yet, for the sake of government, God's established government on earth, the ruler who beareth the sword must not now bear the sword in vain.

Long have I held that war is an enormous crime; long have I regarded all battles as but murder on a large scale; but this time, I, a peaceful man, a follower of the peaceful Savior, do propound war. No, it is not war that I propound, but a just and proper punishment. I will not aid and abet soldiers as *warriors,* but as *executioners* of a lawful sentence, which ought to be executed upon men, who, by the double crime of infamous debauchery, and fearful bloodshed, have brought upon themselves the ban and curse of God; so that they must be punished, or truth and innocence can never walk this earth. As a rule I do not believe in the utility of capital punishment, but the crime has been attended with all the horrid guilt of the cities of the plain, and is too bestial to be endured.

But still, I say, I would cool down the vengeance of Britons, and therefore I would bid you weep. Ye talk of vengeance, but ye know not the men with whom ye have to deal; many a post may come, and many a month run round, and many a year may pass before ye hear of victory over those fierce men. Be not too proud. England talked once of her great deeds, and she hath since been humbled. She may yet again learn that she is not omnipotent.

But ye people of God, weep, weep for this sin that hath broken loose; weep for this hell that hath found its way to earth; go to your chambers and cry out to God to stop this bloodshed. You are to be the saviors of your nation. Not on the bayonets of British soldiery, but on the prayers of British Christians, do we rest. Run to your houses, fall upon your knees; lament most bitterly, for this desperate sin; and then cry to God to save! Remember, he heareth prayer—prayer moveth the arm of the Omnipotent. Let us proclaim a fast; let us gather a solemn assembly; let us cry mightily unto him; let us ask the God of armies to avenge himself; let us pray him so to send the light of the gospel into the land, that such a crime may be impossible a second time; and this time, so to put it down, that it may never have an opportunity of breaking loose again. I know not whether our government will proclaim a national fast; but certain I am it is time that every Christian should celebrate one in his own heart. I bid all of you with whom my word has one atom of respect, if my exhortation has one word of force, I do exhort you to spend special time in prayer just now.

Oh! my friends, ye cannot hear the shrieks, ye have not seen the terror-stricken faces, ye have not beheld the flying fugitives; but you may picture them in your imagination; and he must be accursed who does not pray to God, and lift up his soul in earnest prayer, that he would be pleased now to put his shield between our fellow-subjects and their enemies. And you, especially, the representatives of divers congregations in various parts of this land, give unto God no rest until he be pleased to bestir himself. Make this your cry: "O Lord our God arise, and let thine enemies be scattered, and let all them that hate thee become as the fat of rams." So shall God, through your prayers, haply, establish peace and vindicate justice, and "God, even our own God, shall bless us, and that right early."

## Weeping for the Morally Slain

II. But I have now a greater reason for your sorrow—a more disregarded, and yet more dreadful source of woe. If the first time we said it with plaintive voice, we must a second time say it yet more plaintively—"Oh that my head were waters, and mine eyes a fountain of tears, that I might weep day and night," FOR THE MORALLY SLAIN of the daughter of my people. The old adage is still true, "One-half of the world knows nothing about how the other half lives." A large proportion of you professing Christians have been respectably brought up; you have never in your lives been the visitants of the dens of infamy, you have never frequented the haunts of wickedness, and you know but very little of the sins of your fellow creatures. Perhaps it is well that you should remain as ignorant as you are; for, where to be ignorant is to be free from temptation, it would be folly to be wise.

But there are others who have been obliged to see the wickedness of their fellows; and a public teacher, especially, is bound not to speak from mere hearsay, but to know from authentic sources what is the spirit of the times. It is our business to look with eagle eye through every part of this land, and see what crime is rampant— what kind of crime, and what sort of infamy. Ah, my friends! with all the advancement of piety in this land, with all the hopeful signs of better times, with all the sunlight of glory heralding the coming morn, with all the promises and with all our hopes, we are still obliged to bid you weep because sin aboundeth and iniquity is still mighty. Oh, how many of our sons and daughters, of our friends and relatives, are slain by sin! Ye weep over battle-fields, ye shed tears on the plains of Balaklava; there are worse battlefields than there, and worse deaths than those inflicted by the sword.

Ah, weep ye for the *drunkenness* of this land! How many thousands of our race reel from our gin-palaces into perdition! Oh, if the souls of departed drunkards could be seen at this hour by the Christians of Britain, they would tremble, lift up their hands in sorrow, and begin to weep. My soul might be an everlasting Niobé, perpetually dropping showers of tears, if it might know the doom and the destruction brought on them by that one demon, and by that one demon only! I am no enthusiast, I am no total abstainer.—I do not think the cure of England's drunkenness will come from that quarter. I respect those who thus deny themselves, with a view to the good of others, and should be glad to believe that they accomplish their object. But though I am no total abstainer, I hate drunkenness as much as any man breathing, and have been the means of bringing many poor creatures to relinquish this bestial indulgence. We believe drunkenness to be an awful crime and a horrid sin; we look on all its dreadful effects, and we stand prepared to go to war with it, and to fight side by side with abstainers, even though we may differ from them as to the mode of warfare. Oh, England, how many thousands of thy sons are murdered every year by that accursed devil of drunkenness, that hath such sway over this land!

But there are other crimes too. Alas, for that crime of *debauchery!* What scenes hath the moon seen every night! Sweetly did she shine last evening; the meadows seemed as if they were silvered with beauty when she shone upon them. But ah! what sins were transacted beneath her pale sway! Oh, God, thou only knowest: our hearts might be sickened, and we might indeed cry for "A lodge in some vast wilderness," had we seen what God beheld when he looked down from the moon-lit sky! Ye tell me that sins of that kind are common in the lower class of society. Alas, I know it; alas, how many a girl hath dashed herself into the river to take away her life, because she could not bear the infamy that was brought upon her! But lay not this to the poor; the infamy and sin of our streets begin not with them. It beginneth with the highest ranks—with what we call the noblest classes of society. Men that have defiled themselves and others will stand in our senates, and walk among our peers; men whose characters are not reputable—it is a shame to speak even of the things that are done of them in secret— are received into the drawingrooms and into the parlors of the highest society, while the poor creature who has been the victim of their passions is hooted and cast away!

O Lord God, thou alone knowest the awful ravages that this sin hath made. Thy servant's lips can utter no more than this; he hath gone to the verge of his utterance, he feeleth that he hath no further license in his speech, still he may well cry—"Oh that my head were waters, and mine eyes a fountain of tears, that I might weep day and night for the slain of the daughter of my people!" If ye have walked the hospital, if ye have seen the refuges, if ye have talked with the inmates—and if ye know the gigantic spread of that enormous evil, ye may well sympathize with me when I say, that at the thought of it my spirit is utterly cast down. I feel that I would rather die than live whilst sin thus reigns and iniquity thus spreads.

But are these the only evils? Are these the only demons that are devouring our people? Ah, would to God it were so. Behold, throughout this land, how are men falling by every sin, disguised as it is under the shape of pleasure. Have ye never, as from some distant journey ye have returned to your houses at midnight, seen the multitudes of people who are turning out of casinos, low theaters, and other houses of sin? I do not frequent those places, nor from earliest childhood have I ever trodden those floors; but, from the company that I have seen issuing from these dens, I could only lift up my hands, and pray God to close such places; they seem to be the gates of hell, and their doors, as they very properly themselves say, "Lead to the pit."

Ah, may God be pleased to raise up many who shall warn this city, and bid Christian people cry day and night "for the slain of the daughter of our people!" Christians, never leave off weeping for men's sins and infamies. There are sins by day; God's own day, this day is defiled, is broken in pieces and trodden under foot. There are sins every morning committed, and sins each night. If ye could see them ye might be never happy, if ye could walk in the midst of them and behold them with your eyes, if God would give you grace, ye might perpetually weep, for ye would always have cause for sorrow. "Oh that my head were waters, and mine eyes a fountain of tears, that I might weep day and night for the slain of the daughter of my people."

## Weeping for Those Without Christ

But now I must just throw in something which will more particularly apply to you. Perhaps I have very few here who would indulge in open and known sin; perhaps most of you belong to the good and amiable class who have every kind of virtue, and of whom it must be said, "One thing thou lackest." My heart never feels so grieved as at the sight of you. How often have I been entertained most courteously and hospitably, as the Lord's servant, in the houses of men and of women whose characters are supremely excellent, who have every virtue that could adorn a Christian, except faith in the Lord Jesus Christ; who might be held up as the very mirrors and patterns to be imitated by others. How has my heart grieved when I have thought of these, still undecided, still godless, prayerless and Christless. I have many of you in this congregation to-day—I could not put my finger upon one solitary fault in your character; you are scrupulously correct in your morals—Alas, alas, alas for you, that you should still be dead in trespasses and sins, because you have not been renewed by divine grace! So lovely, and yet without faith; so beautiful, so admirable, and yet not converted.

O God, when drunkards die, when swearers perish, when harlots and seducers sink to the fate they have earned, we may well weep for such sinners; but when these who have walked in our midst and have almost been acknowledged as believers, are cast away because they lack the one thing needful, it seems enough to make angels weep. O members of churches, ye may well take up the cry of Jeremiah when ye remember what multitudes of these you have in your midst—men who have a name to live and are dead: and others, who though they profess not to be Christians, are almost persuaded to obey their Lord and Master, but are yet not partakers of the divine life of God.

But now I shall want, if I can, to press this pathetic subject a little further upon your minds. In the day when Jeremiah wept this lamentation with an exceeding loud and bitter cry, Jerusalem was in all her mirth and merriment. Jeremiah was a sad man in the midst of a multitude of merry makers; he told them that Jerusalem should be destroyed, that their temple should become a heap, and Nebuchadnezzar should lay it with the ground. They laughed him to scorn; they mocked him. Still the viol and the dance were only to be seen. Do you not picture that brave old man, for he was bravely plaintive, sitting down in the courts of the Temple? And though as yet the pillars were unfallen, and the golden roof was yet unstained, he lifted up his hands and pictured to himself this scene of Jerusalem's Temple burned with fire, her women and her children carried away captive, and her sons given to the sword. And when he pictured this, he did, as it were, in spirit set himself down upon one of the broken pillars of the Temple, and there, in the midst of desolation which was not as yet— but which faith, the evidence of things not seen, did picture to him—cry, "Oh that my head were waters, and mine eyes a fountain of tears."

And now, to-day, here are many of you masquers and

merry makers in this ball of life; ye are here merry and glad to-day, and ye marvel that I should talk of you as persons for whom we ought to weep. "Weep ye for me!" you say; "I am in health, I am in riches, I am enjoying life; why weep for me? I need none of your sentimental weeping!" Ah, but we weep because we foresee the future. If you could live here always, we might not, perhaps, weep for you; but we, by the eye of faith, look forward to the time when the pillars of heaven must totter, when this earth must shake, when death must give up its prey, when the great white throne must be set in the clouds of heaven, and the thunders and lightnings of Jehovah shall be launched in armies, and the angels of God shall be marshalled in their ranks, to swell the pomp of the grand assize—we look forward to that hour, and by faith we see you standing before the Judge; we see his eye sternly fixed on you; we hear him read the book; we mark your tottering knee, whilst sentence after sentence of thundering wrath strikes on your appalled ear; we think we see your blanched countenances; we mark your terror beyond all description, when he cries, "Depart, ye cursed!" We hear your shrieks; we hear you cry, "Rocks hide us; mountains on us fall!" We see the angel with fiery brand pursuing you; we hear your last unutterable shriek of woe as you descend into the pit of hell— and we ask you if you could see this as we see it, would you wonder that at the thought of your destruction we are prepared to weep? "Oh that my head were waters, and mine eyes were a fountain of tears that I might weep" over you who will not stand in the judgment, but must be driven away like chaff into the unquenchable fire!

And by the eye of faith we look further than that; we look into the grim and awful future: our faith looks through the gate of iron bound with adamant; we see the place of the condemned; our ear, opened by faith, hears "The sullen groans, and hollow moans, and shrieks of tortured ghosts!" Our eye anointed with heavenly eye salve, sees the worm that never dieth, it beholds the fire that never can be quenched, and sees you writhing in the flame!

O professors, if ye believed not in the wrath to come, and in hell eternal, I should not wonder that ye were unmoved by such a thought as this. But if ye believe what your Savior said when he declared that he would destroy both body and soul in hell, I must wonder that ye could endure the thought without weeping for your fellow-creatures who are going there. If I saw mine enemy marching into the flames, I would rush between him and the fire and seek to preserve him; and will you see men and women marching on in a mad career of vice and sin, well aware that "the wages of sin is death," and will you not interpose so much as a tear? What! are you more brutal than the beast, more stolid than the stone! It must be so, if the thought of the unutterable torment of hell, doth not draw tears from your eyes and prayer from your hearts. Oh, if to-day some strong archangel could unbolt the gates of hell, and for a solitary second permit the voice of wailing and weeping to come up to our ears; oh, how should we grieve! Each man would put his hand upon his loins and walk this earth in terror. That shriek might make each hair stand on an end upon our heads, and then make us roll ourselves in the dust for anguish and woe—

> Oh, doleful state of dark despair,
> When God has far removed,
> And fixed their dreadful station where

They must not taste his love.

Oh that my head were waters, and mine eyes a fountain of tears, that I might weep for some of you that are going there this day.

Remember, again, O Christian, that those for whom we ask you to weep this day are persons who have had great privilege, and consequently, if lost, must expect greater punishment. I do not to-day ask your sympathies for men in foreign lands; I shall not bid you weep for Hottentots or Mahomedans though ye might weep for them, and ye have goodly cause to do so—but I ask this day your tears for the slain of the daughter of your own people. Oh! what multitudes of heathens we have in all our places of worship! what multitudes of unconverted persons in all the pews of the places where we usually assemble to worship God; and I may add, what hundreds we have here who are without God, without Christ, without hope in the world. And these are not like Hottentots who have not heard the Word: they have heard it, and they have rejected it.

Many of you, when you die, cannot plead, as an excuse, that you did not know your duty; you heard it plainly preached to you, you heard it in every corner of the streets, you had the book of God in your houses. You cannot say that you did not know what you must do to be saved. You read the Bible, you understand salvation—many of you are deeply taught in the theory of salvation; when ye perish, your blood must be of your own head, and the Master may well cry over you to-day, "Woe unto thee, Bethsaida, woe unto thee, Chorazin! For if the mighty works that were done in thee, had been done in Tyre and Sidon, they would have repented long ago in sackcloth and ashes."

I wonder at myself this day; I hate my eyes, I feel as if I could pluck them from their sockets now, because they will not weep as I desire, over poor souls who are perishing! How many have I among you whom I love and who love me! We are no strangers to one another, we could not live at a distance from each other, our hearts have been joined together long and firmly. Ye have stood by me in the hour of tribulation; ye have listened to the Word, ye have been pleased with it; I bear you witness that if you could pluck out your eyes for me you would do it. And yet I know there are many of you true lovers of God's Word in appearance, and certainly great lovers of God's servant; but alas for you, that you should still be in the gall of bitterness and in the bonds of iniquity! Alas, my sister, I can weep for thee! Woe, woe, my brother, I can weep for thee! we have met together in God's house, we have prayed together, and yet we must be sundered. Shepherd, some of thy flock will perish! O sheep of my pasture, people of my care, must I have that horrid thought upon me, that I must lose you? Must we, at the day of judgment, say farewell for ever? Must I bear my witness against you?

I shall be honest; I have dealt faithfully with your souls. God is my witness, I have often preached in weakness; often have I had to groan before him that I have not preached as I could desire; but I have never preached insincerely. Nobody will ever dare to accuse me of dishonesty in this respect; not one of your smiles have I ever courted. I have never dreaded your frowns; I have been in weariness oftentimes, when I should have rested, preaching God's Word. But what of that? That were nothing; only this much, there is some responsibility resting upon you. And remember, that to perish under the sound of the Gospel is to perish more terribly than anywhere else.

But, my hearers, must that be your lot? And must I be witness against you in the day of judgment? I pray God it may not be so; I beseech the Master, that he may spare us each such a fate as that.

## Weeping for Our Families

And now, dear friends, I have one word to add before I leave this point. Some of you need not look round on this congregation to find cause for weeping. My pious brethren and sisters, you have cause enough to weep in your own families. Ah, mother! I know thy griefs; thou hast had cause to cry to God with weeping eyes for many a mournful hour, because of thy son; thine offspring hath turned against thee; and he that came forth of thee has despised his mother's God. Father, thou hast carefully brought up thy daughter; thou hast nourished her when she was young, and taken her fondly in thine arms; she was the delight of thy life, yet she hath sinned against thee and against God. Many of you have sons and daughters that you often mention in your prayers, but never with hope. You have often thought that God has said of your son, "Ephraim is given to idols; let him alone;" the child of your affection has become an adder stinging your heart! Oh, then weep, I beseech you. Parents, do not leave off weeping for your children; do not become hardened towards them, sinners though they be; it may be that God may yet bring them to himself.

It was but last church meeting that we received into our communion a young friend who was educated and brought up by a pious minister in Colchester. She had been there many years, and when she came away to London the minister said to her, "Now, my girl, I have prayed for you hundreds of times, and I have done all I can with you; your heart is as hard as a stone; I must leave you with God!" That broke her heart, she is now converted to Jesus. How many sons and daughters have made their parents feel the same! "There," they have said, "I must leave you; I cannot do more." But in saying that, they have not meant that they would leave them unwept for; but they have thought within themselves, that if they were damned, they would follow them weeping to the very gates of hell, if by tears they could decoy them into heaven.

How can a man be a Christian, and not love his off-spring? How can a man be a believer in Jesus Christ, and yet have a cold and hard heart in the things of the kingdom, towards his children? I have heard of ministers of a certain sect, and professors of a certain class, who have despised family prayer, who have laughed at family god-liness and thought nothing of it. I cannot understand how the men can know as much as they do about the gospel, and yet have so little of the spirit of it. I pray God, deliver you and deliver me from anything like that. No, it is our business to train up our children in the fear of the Lord; and though we cannot give them grace, it is ours to pray to the God who can give it; and in answer to our many supplications, he will not turn us away, but he will be pleased to take notice of our prayers and to regard our sighs.

And now, Christian mourners, I have given you work enough; may God the Holy Spirit enable you to do it. Let me exhort you, yet once again, to weep. Do you need a copy? Behold your Master; he has come to the brow of the hill; he sees Jerusalem lying on the hill opposite to him; he looks down upon it, as he sees it there—beautiful for situation, the joy of the whole earth—instead of feel-ing the rapture of an artist who surveys the ramparts of a strong city, and marks the position of some magnificent tower in the midst of glorious scenery, he bursts out, and he cries, "O Jerusalem, Jerusalem! how often would I have gathered thy children together as a hen gathereth her chickens under her wings, but ye would not. Behold, your house is left unto you desolate."

Go ye now your ways, and as ye stand on any of the hills around, and beheld this Behemoth city lying in the valley, say, "O London, London! how great thy guilt. Oh, that the Master would gather thee under his wing, and make thee his city, the joy of the whole earth! O London, London! full of privileges, and full of sin; exalted to heaven by the gospel, thou shalt be cast down to hell by thy rejection of it!" And then, when ye have wept over London, go and weep over the street in which you live, as you see the sabbath broken, and God's laws trampled upon, and men's bodies profaned—go ye and weep! Weep, for the court in which you live in your humble poverty; weep for the square in which you live in your magnificent wealth; weep for the humbler street in which you live in competence; weep for your neighbors and your friends, lest any of them, having lived godless, may die godless! Then go to your house, weep for your family, for your servants, for your husband, for your wife, for your children. Weep, weep; cease not weeping, till God hath renewed them by his Spirit. And if you have any friends with whom you sinned in your past life, be earnest for their salvation.

George Whitefield said there were many young men with whom he played at cards, in his lifetime, and spent hours in wasting his time when he ought to have been about other business; and when he was converted, his first thought was, "I must by God's grace have these converted too." And he never rested, till he could say, that he did not know of one of them, a companion of his guilt, who was not now a companion with him in the tribulation of the gospel.

Oh, let it be so with you! Nor let your exertions end in tears; mere weeping will do nothing without action. Get you on your feet; ye that have voices and might, go forth and preach the gospel, preach it in every street and lane of this huge city; ye that have wealth, go forth and spend it for the poor, and sick, and needy, and dying, the uneducated, the unenlightened; ye that have time, go forth and spend it in deeds and goodness; ye that have power in prayer, go forth and pray; ye that can handle the pen, go forth and write down iniquity—every one to his post, every one of you to your gun in this day of battle; now for God and for his truth; for God and for the right; let every one of us who knows the Lord seek to fight under his banner! O God, without whom all our exertions are vain, come now and stir up thy church to greater diligence and more affectionate earnestness, that we may not have in future such cause to weep as we have this day! Sinners, believe on the Lord Jesus; he hath died; look to him and live, and God the Almighty bless you! To God the Father, Son, and Holy Ghost, be glory for ever and ever.

*"The Greatest Wonder of All"* is taken from Seven Wonders of Grace, *a posthumous collection of Spurgeon's works devoted to exploring the wonders of God's grace. Here Spurgeon uses a passage from Ezekiel to delineate the nature of the doom from which God's grace delivers men and describe how this grace proceeds. Spurgeon concludes with a plea to his reader to consider his own situation before God, in light of the coming judgment.*

CHAPTER SEVEN

# The Greatest Wonder of All

*And I was left (Ezek. 9:8).*

$S$alvation never shines so brightly to any man's eyes as when it comes to himself. Then is grace illustrious indeed when we can see it working with divine power upon ourselves. To our apprehension, our own case is ever the most desperate, and mercy shown to us is the most extraordinary. We see others perish, and wonder that the same doom has not befallen ourselves. The horror of the ruin which we dreaded, and our intense delight at the certainty of safety in Christ unite with our personal sense of unworthiness to make us cry in amazement, "And I was left."

Ezekiel, in vision, saw the slaughtermen smiting right and left at the bidding of divine justice, and as he stood unharmed among the heaps of the slain, he exclaimed with surprise, "I was left." It may be, the day will come when we, too, shall cry with solemn joy, "And I, too, by sovereign grace, am spared while others perish." Special grace will cause us to marvel. Especially will it be so at the last dread day.

Read the story of the gross idolatry of the people of Jerusalem, as recorded in the eighth chapter of Ezekiel's prophecy, and you will not wonder at the judgment with which the Lord at length overthrew the city. Let us set our hearts to consider how the Lord dealt with the guilty people. "Six men came from the way of the higher gate, which lieth toward the north, and every man with a slaughter weapon in his hand." The destruction wrought by these executioners was swift and terrible, and it was typical of other solemn visitations. All through history the observing eye notices lines of justice, red marks upon the page where the Judge of all the earth has at last seen it needful to decree a terrible visitation upon a guilty people.

All these past displays of divine vengeance point at a coming judgment even more complete and overwhelming. The past is prophetic of the future. A day is surely coming when the Lord Jesus, who came once to save, will descend a second time to judge. Despised mercy has always been succeeded by deserved wrath, and so must it be in the end of all things. "But who may abide the day of his coming? or who shall stand when he appeareth?" When sinners are smitten, who will be left? He shall lift the balances of justice, and make bare the sword of execution. When his avenging angels shall gather the vintage of the earth, who among us shall exclaim in wondering gratitude, "And I was left"? Such an one will be a wonder of grace indeed; worthy to take rank with those marvels of grace of whom we have spoken in the former discourses of this book. Reader, will you be an instance of sparing grace, and cry, "And I was left"?

## The Character of the Doom

We will use the wonderfully descriptive vision of this chapter that we may with holy fear behold *the character of the doom* from which grace delivers us, and then we will dwell upon the exclamation of our text, "I was left," considering it as the joyful utterance of *the persons who are privileged to escape the destruction.*

By the help of the Holy Spirit, let us first solemnly consider THE TERRIBLE DOOM from which the prophet in vision saw himself preserved, regarding it as a figure of the judgment which is yet to come upon all the world.

Observe, first, that it was a *just* punishment inflicted upon those who had been often warned; a punishment which they wilfully brought upon themselves. God had said that if they set up idols he would destroy them, for he would not endure such an insult to his Godhead. He had often pleaded with them, not with words only, but with severe providences, for their land had been laid desolate, their city had been besieged, and their kings had been carried away captive; but they were bent on backsliding to the worship of their idol gods. Therefore, when the sword of the Lord was drawn from its scabbard, it was no novel punishment, no freak of vengeance, no unexpected execution.

So, in the close of life, and at the end of the world, when judgment comes on men, it will be just and according to the solemn warnings of the word of God. When I read the terrible things which are written in God's book in reference to future punishment, especially the awful things which Jesus spoke concerning the place where their worm dieth not and their fire is not quenched, I am greatly pressed in spirit. Some there be who sit in judg-

CHARLES H. SPURGEON: THE BEST FROM ALL HIS WORKS

ment upon the great Judge, and condemn the punishment which he inflicts as too severe. As for myself, I cannot measure the power of God's anger, but let it burn as it may, I am sure that it will be just. No needless pang will be inflicted upon a single one of God's creatures: even those who are doomed for ever will endure no more than justice absolutely requires, no more than they themselves would admit to be the due reward of their sins, if their consciences would judge aright.

Mark you, this is the very hell of hell that men will know that they are justly suffering. To endure a tyrant's wrath would be a small thing compared with suffering what one has brought upon himself by wilful wanton choice of wrong. Sin and suffering are indissolubly bound together in the constitution of nature; it cannot be otherwise, nor ought it to be. It is right that evil should be punished. Those who were punished in Jerusalem could not turn upon the executioners and say, "We do not deserve this doom;" but every cruel wound of the Chaldean sword and every fierce crash of the Babylonian battle-axe fell on men who in their consciences knew that they were only reaping what they themselves had sown. Brethren, what wonders of grace shall we be if from a judgment which we have so richly deserved we shall be rescued at the last!

## Slaughter Was Preceded by Separation

Let us notice very carefully that this slaughter was *preceded by a separation* which removed from among the people those who were distinct in character. Before the slaughtermen proceeded to their stern task a man appeared among them clothed in linen with a writer's inkhorn by his side, who marked all those who in their hearts were grieved at the evil done in the city. Until these were marked the destroyers did not commence their work. Whenever the Lord lays bare his arm for war he first gathers his saints into a place of safety. He did not destroy the world by the flood till Noah and his family were safe in the ark. He would not suffer a single fire-drop to fall on Sodom till Lot had escaped to Zoar. He carefully preserves his own; nor flood nor flame, nor pestilence nor famine shall do them ill. We read in Revelation that the angel said, "Hurt not the earth, neither the sea, nor the trees, till we have sealed the servants of our God in their foreheads."

Vengeance must sheathe her sword, till love has housed its darlings. When Christ cometh to destroy the earth, he will first catch away his people. Ere the elements shall melt with fervent heat, and the pillars of the universe shall rock and reel beneath the weight of wrathful deity, he will have caught up his elect into the air so that they shall be ever with the Lord. When he cometh he shall divide the nations as a shepherd divideth his sheep from the goats; no sheep of his shall be destroyed: he shall without fail take the tares from among the wheat, but not one single ear of wheat shall be in danger.

O that we may be among the selected ones and prove his power to keep us in the day of wrath. May each one of us say amid the wreck of matter and the crash of worlds, "And I was left." Dear friend, are you marked in the forehead, think you? If at this moment my voice were drowned by the trumpet of resurrection, would you be amongst those who awake to safety and glory? Would you be able to say, "The multitude perished around me, but I was left"? It will be so if you hate the sins by which you are surrounded, and if you have received the mark of the blood of Jesus upon your souls; if not, you will not escape, for there is no other door of salvation but his saving name. God grant us grace to belong to that chosen number who wear the covenant seal, the mark of him who counteth up the people.

## Judgment Was Placed in the Mediator's Hands

Next, this judgment was placed *in the Mediator's hands*. I want you to notice this. Observe that, according to the chapter, there was no slaughter done except where the man with the writer's inkhorn led the way. So again we read in the tenth chapter, that "One cherub stretched forth his hand from between the cherubims unto the fire that was between the cherubims, and took thereof and put it into the hands of him that was clothed with linen; who took it, and went out," and cast it over the city. See you this. God's glory of old shone forth between the cherubim, that is to say, over the place of propitiation and atonement, and as long as that glow of light remained no judgment fell on Jerusalem, for God in Christ condemns not. But by-and-by "The glory of the God of Israel was gone up from the cherub, whereupon he was, to the threshold of the house," and then judgment was near to come. When God no longer deals with men in Christ his wrath burns like fire, and he commissions the ambassador of mercy to be the messenger of wrath. The very man who marked with his pen the saved ones threw burning coals upon the city and led the way for the destruction of the sinful.

What does this teach but this—"The Father judgeth no man, but hath committed all judgment unto the Son"? I know of no truth more dreadful to meditate upon. Think of it, ye careless ones: the very Christ who died on Calvary is he by whom you will be sentenced.

God will judge the world by this man Christ Jesus: he it is that will come in the clouds of heaven, and before him shall be gathered all nations; and when those who have despised him shall look upon his face they will be terrified beyond conception. Not the lightnings, not the thunders, not the dreadful sound of the last tremendous trump shall so alarm them as that face of injured love. Then will they cry to the mountains and hills to hide them from the face of him that sitteth upon the throne.

Why, it is the face of him that wept for sinners, the face which scoffers stained with bloody drops extracted by the thorny crown, the face of the incarnate God who, in infinite mercy, came to save mankind! But because they have despised him, because they would not be saved, because they preferred their own lusts to infinite love, and would persist in rejecting God's best proof of kindness, therefore will they say, "Hide us from the face," for the sight of that face shall be to them more accusing, and more condemning, than all else besides. How dreadful is this truth! The more you consider it, the more will it fill your soul with terror! Would to God it might drive you to fly to Jesus, for then you will behold him with joy in that day.

## Destruction Began at the Sanctuary

This destruction, we are told, *began at the sanctuary.* Suppose the Lord were to visit London in his anger, where would he begin to smite? "Oh," somebody says, "of course the destroying angel would go down to the low music halls and dancing rooms, or he would sweep out the back slums and the drink palaces, the jails and places where women of ill life do congregate." Turn to the Scripture which surrounds our text. The Lord says,

"Begin at my sanctuary." Begin at the churches, begin at the chapels, begin at the church members, begin at the ministers, begin at the bishops, begin at those who are teachers of the gospel. Begin at the chief and front of the religious world, begin at the high professors who are looked up to as examples. What does Peter say? "The time is come that judgment must begin at the house of God: and if it first begin at us, what shall the end be of them that obey not the gospel of God? And if the righteous scarcely be saved, where shall the ungodly and the sinner appear?"

The first thing the slaughtermen did was to slay the ancient men which were before the temple, even the seventy elders of the people, for they were secret idolaters. You may be sure that the sword which did not spare the chief men and fathers made but short work with the baser sort. Elders of our churches, ministers of Christ, judgment will begin with us; we must not expect to find more lenient treatment than others at the last great assize; nay, rather, if there shall be a specially careful testing of sincerity it will be for us who have taken upon ourselves to lead others to the Savior.

For this cause let us see well to it that we be not deceived or deceivers, for we shall surely be detected in that day. To play the hypocrite is to play the fool. Will a man deceive his Maker, or delude the Most High? It cannot be. You church members, all of you, should look well to it, for judgment will begin with you. God's fire is in Zion and his furnace in Jerusalem.

In the olden time the people fled to churches and holy places for sanctuary; but how vain will this be when the Lord's avengers shall come forth, since there the havoc will begin! How fiercely shall the sword sweep through the hosts of carnal professors, the men who called themselves servants of God, while they were slaves of the devil; who drank of the cup of the Lord but were drunken with the wine of their own lusts: who could lie and cheat and commit fornication, and yet dared to approach the sacred table of the Lord? What cutting and hewing will there be among the base-born professors of our churches! It were better for such men that they had never been born, or, being born, that their lot had fallen amid heathen ignorance, so that they might have been unable to add sin to sin by lying unto the living God. "Begin at my sanctuary." The word is terrible to all those who have a name to live and are dead. God grant that in such testing times when many fail we may survive every ordeal and through grace exclaim in the end, "And I was left."

## Only Those with the Mark Were Spared

After the executioners had begun at the sanctuary it is to be observed that they *did not spare any except those upon whom was the mark.* Old and young, men and women, priests and people, all were slain who had not the sacred sign; and so in the last tremendous day all sinners who have not fled to Christ will perish. Our dear babes that died in infancy we believe to be all washed in the blood of Jesus and all saved; but for the rest of mankind who have lived to years of responsibility there will be only one of two things—they must either be saved because they had faith in Christ, or else the full weight of divine wrath must fall upon them.

Either the mark of Christ's pen or of Christ's sword must be upon every one. There will be no sparing of one man because he was rich, nor of another because he was learned, nor of a third because he was eloquent, nor of a fourth because he was held in high esteem. Those who are marked with the blood of Christ are safe! Without that mark all are lost! This is the one separating sign— do you wear it? Or will you die in your sins? Bow down at once before the feet of Jesus and beseech him to mark you as his own, that so you may be one of those who will joyfully cry, "And I was left."

## The Nature of Those Who Escaped

Now, secondly, I have to call your very particular attention to THE PERSONS WHO ESCAPED, who could each say, "And I was left." We are told that those were marked for mercy who did "sigh and cry for the abominations that were done in the midst thereof." Now we must be very particular about this. It is no word of mine, remember: it is God's word, and therefore I beg you to hear and weigh it for yourselves. We do not read that the devouring sword passed by those quiet people who never did anybody any harm: no mention is made of such an exemption. Neither does the record say that the Lord saved those professors who were judicious, and maintained a fair name and repute until death.

No; the only people that were saved were those who were exercised in heart, and that heart-work was of a painful kind: they sighed and cried because of abounding sin. They saw it, protested against it, avoided it, and last of all wept over it continually. Where testimony failed it remained for them to mourn; retiring from public labors they sat them down and sighed their hearts away because of the evils which they could not cure; and when they felt that sighing alone would do no good they took to crying in prayer to God that he would come and put an end of the dreadful ills which brooded over the land.

I would not say a hard thing, but I wonder, if I were able to read the secret lives of professors of religion whether I should find that they all sigh and cry over the sins of others? Are the tenth of them thus engaged? I am afraid that it does not cause some people much anxiety when they see sin rampant around them. They say that they are sorry, but it never frets them much, or causes them as much trouble as would come of a lost sixpence or a cut finger.

Did you ever feel as if your heart would break over an ungodly son? I do not believe that you are a Christian man if you have such a son and have not felt an agony on his behalf. Did you ever feel as if you could lay down your life to save that daughter of yours? I cannot believe that you are a Christian woman if you have not sometimes come to that. When you have gone through the street and heard an oath, has not your blood chilled in you? has not horror taken hold upon you because of the wicked? There cannot be much grace in you if that has not been the case. If you can go up and down in the world fully at ease because you are prospering in business, and things go smoothly with you, if you forget the woe of this city's sin and poverty, and the yet greater woe which cometh upon it, how dwelleth the love of God in you? The saving mark is only set on those who sigh and cry, and if you are heartless and indifferent there is no such mark on you.

"Are we to be always miserable?" asks one. Far from it. There are many other things to make us rejoice, but if the sad state of our fellow men does not cause us to sigh and cry, then we have not the grace of God in us. "Well," says one, "but every man must look to himself." That is the language of Cain—"Am I my brother's keeper?" That kind of talk is in keeping with the spirit of the wicked one and his seed, but the heir of heaven abhors such language. The genuine Christian loves his race, and therefore he longs to see it made holy and happy. He cannot bear to see men sinning, and so dishonoring God and ruining themselves. If we really love the Lord we shall sometimes lie awake at night sighing to think how his name is blasphemed, and how little progress his gospel makes. We shall groan to think that men should despise the glorious God who made them, and who daily loads them with benefits. . . .

But it was not their mourning which saved those who escaped—it was the mark which they all received which preserved them from destruction. We must all bear the mark of Jesus Christ. What is that? It is the mark of faith in the atoning blood. That sets apart the chosen of the Lord, and that alone. If you have that mark—and you have it not unless you sigh and cry over the sins of others—then in that last day no sword of justice can come near you. Did you read that word, "But come not nigh any man upon whom is the mark." Come not even near the marked ones lest they be afraid. The grace-marked man is safe even from the near approach of ill. Christ bled for him, and therefore he cannot, must not, die. Let him alone, ye bearers of the destroying weapons. Just as the angel of death, when he flew through the land of Egypt, was forbidden to touch a house where the blood of the lamb was on the lintel and the two side posts, so is it sure that avenging justice cannot touch the man who is in Christ Jesus. Who is he that condemneth since Christ has died?

Have you, then, the blood mark? Yes or no. Do not

refuse to question yourself upon this point. Do not take it for granted, lest you be deceived. Believe me, your all hangs upon it. If you are not registered by the man clothed in linen you will not be able to say, "And I was left."

## Humility in Those Who Were Left

This brings me to this last point which I desire to speak of. *What were the prophet's emotions when he said, "And I was left"?* He saw men falling right and left, and *he* himself stood like a lone rock amidst a sea of blood; and he cried in wonder, "And I was left."

Let us hear what he further says—"I fell on my face." He lay prostrate with *humility*. Have you a hope that you are saved? Fall on your face, then! See the hell from which you are delivered, and bow before the Lord. Why are you to be saved more than anyone else? Certainly not because of any merit in you. It is due to the sovereign grace of God alone. Fall on your face and own your indebtedness.

> Why was I made to hear thy voice,
> And enter while there's room,
> When thousands make a wretched choice,
> And rather starve than come?

"And I was left."

If a man has been a drunkard, and has at length been led to flee to Christ, when he says, "And I was left," he will feel the hot tears rising to his eyes, for many other drinkers have died in delirium. One who has been a public sinner, when she is saved will not be able to think of it without astonishment. Indeed, each saved man is a mar-

CHARLES H. SPURGEON: THE BEST FROM ALL HIS WORKS

vel to himself. Nobody here wonders more at divine grace in his salvation than I do myself. Why was I chosen, and called, and saved? I cannot make it out, and I never shall; but I will always praise, and bless, and magnify my Lord for casting an eye of love upon me. Will you not do the same, beloved, if you feel that you by grace are left? Will you not fall on your face and bless the mercy which makes you to differ?

What did the prophet do next? Finding that he was left he began to pray for others. "Ah, Lord," said he, "wilt thou destroy all the residue of Israel?" Intercession is an instinct of the renewed heart. When the believer finds that he is safe he must pray for his fellow-men. Though the prophet's prayer was too late, yet, blessed be God, ours will not be. We shall be heard. Pray, then, for perishing men. Ask God, who has spared you, to spare those who are like you.

Somebody has said, there will be three great wonders in heaven, first, to see so many there whom we never expected to meet in glory; secondly, to miss so many of whom we felt sure that they must be safe; and thirdly, the greatest wonder of all will be to find ourselves there. I am sure that everyone who has a hope of being in glory feels it to be a marvel; and he resolves, "If I am saved, I will sing the loudest of them all, for I shall owe most to the abounding mercy of God."

## Who Will Be Left?

Let me ask a few questions, and I have done. The first—and let each man ask it of himself—shall I be left when the ungodly are slain? Answer it now to yourselves. Men, women, children, will you be spared in that last great day? Are you in Christ? Have you a good hope in him? Do not lie unto yourselves. You will be weighed in the balances; will you be found wanting or not? "Shall I be left?" Let that question burn into your souls.

Next, will my relatives be saved? My wife, my husband, my children, my brother, my sister, my father, my mother—will these all be saved? Happy are we who can say, "Yes, we believe they will," as some of us can joyfully hope. But if you have to say, "No, I fear that my boy is unconverted, or that my father is unsaved;" then do not rest till you have wrestled with God for their salvation. Good woman, if you are obliged to say, "I fear my husband is unconverted," join me in prayer. Bow your heads at once and cry unto your God, "Lord, save our children! Lord, save our parents! Lord, save our husbands and wives, our brothers and sisters; and let the whole of our families meet in heaven, unbroken circles, for thy name's sake!"

May God hear that prayer if it has come from the lips of sincerity! I could not endure the thought of missing one of my boys in heaven: I hope I shall see them both there, and therefore I am in deep sympathy with any of you who have not seen your households brought to Christ. O for grace to pray earnestly and labor zealously for the salvation of your whole households.

The next earnest enquiry is, if you and your relatives are saved, how about your neighbors, your fellow-workmen, your companions in business? "Oh," say you, "many of them are scoffers. A good many of them are still in the gall of bitterness." A sorrowful fact, but have you spoken to them? It is wonderful what a kind word will do. Have you tried it? Did you ever try to speak to that person who meets you every morning as you go to work? Suppose he should be lost! Oh, it will be a bitter feeling for you to think that he went down to the pit without your making an effort to bring him to God. Do not let it be so.

"But we must not be too pushing," says one. I do not know about that. If you saw poor people in a burning house nobody would blame you for being officious if you helped to save them. When a man is sinking in the river, if you jump in and pull him out nobody will say, "You were rude and intrusive, for you were never introduced to him!" This world has been lost, and it must be saved; and we must not mind manners in saving it. We must get a grip of sinking sinners somehow, even if it be by the hair of their heads, ere they sink, for if they sink they are lost for ever. They will forgive us very soon for any roughness that we use; but we shall not forgive ourselves if, for want of a little energy, we permit them to die without a knowledge of the truth.

Oh, beloved friends, if you are left while others perish, I beseech you, by the mercies of God, by the bowels of compassion which are in Christ Jesus, by the bleeding wounds of the dying Son of God, do love your fellow men, and sigh and cry about them if you cannot bring them to Christ. If you cannot save them you can weep over them. If you cannot give them a drop of cold water in hell, you can give them your heart's tears while yet they are in this body.

But are you in very deed reconciled to God yourselves? Reader, are you cured of the awful disease of sin? Are you marked with the blood-red sign of trust in the atoning blood? Do you believe in the Lord Jesus Christ? If not, the Lord have mercy upon you! May you have sense enough to have mercy upon yourself. May the Spirit of God instruct you to that end. Amen.

As a corollary of Spurgeon's fervent evangelistic message of grace, he was supremely concerned with how men may most effectively be reached with the gospel of grace. "Qualifications for Soul-Winning—Manward" is taken from Spurgeon's The Soul Winner *and immediately succeeds* "Qualifications for Soul-Winning—Godward." *Spurgeon's advice is always compelling and practical and is sound advice for every believer, even when not specifically engaged in* "soul-winning" *activities.*

CHAPTER EIGHT

# Qualifications for Soul-Winning—Manward

You remember, brethren, that on the last occasion when I gave you a lecture on soul-winning, I spoke of the qualifications, Godward, that would fit a man to be a soul-winner; and I tried to describe to you the kind of man that the Lord was most likely to use in the winning of souls. This afternoon, I propose to take as my subject—

## THE CHARACTERISTICS OF A SOUL-WINNER, MANWARD.

I might almost mention the very same points that I enumerated before as being those which will best tell manward, for I do think that those qualities that commend themselves to the notice of God, as being most adapted to the end He desires, are also likely to be approved by the object acted upon, that is, the soul of man.

## Intelligence

There have been many men in the world who have not been at all adapted for this work; and, first, let me say that *an ignoramus is not likely to be much of a soul-winner.* A man who only knows that he is a sinner, and that Christ is a Savior, may be very useful to others in the same condition as himself, and it is his duty to do the best he can with what little knowledge he possesses; but, on the whole, I should not expect such a man to be very largely used in the service of God. If he had enjoyed a wider and deeper experience of the things of God, if he had been in the highest sense a learned man because taught of God, he could have used his knowledge for the good of others; but being to a great extent ignorant of the things of God himself, I do not see how he can make them known to other people. Truly, there must be some light in that candle which is to lighten men's darkness, and *there must be some information in that man who is to be a teacher of his fellows.* The man who is almost or altogether ignorant, whatever will he has to do good, must be left out of the race of great soul-winners; he is disqualified from even entering the lists, and therefore, let us all ask, brethren, that we may be well instructed in the truth of God, that we may be able to teach others also.

## Sincerity

Granted that you are not of the ignorant class to which I have been referring, but supposing that you are well instructed in the best of all wisdom, what are the qualities that you must have towards men if you are to win them for the Lord? I should say, there must be about us *an evident sincerity;* not only sincerity, but such sincerity that it shall be manifest at once to anyone who honestly looks for it. It must be quite clear to your hearers that you have a firm belief in the truths that you are preaching; otherwise, you will never make them believe them. Unless they are convinced, beyond all question, that you do believe these truths yourselves, there will be no efficacy and no force in your preaching. No one must suspect you of proclaiming to others what you do not fully believe in yourself; if it should ever be so, your work will be of no effect. All who listen to you ought to be conscious that you are exercising one of the noblest crafts, and performing one of the most sacred functions that ever fell to the lot of man. If you have only a feeble appreciation of the gospel you profess to deliver, it is impossible for those who hear your proclamation of it to be greatly influenced by it.

I heard it asked, the other day, of a certain minister, "Did he preach a good sermon?" and the reply to the enquiry was, "What he *said* was very good." "But did you not profit by the sermon?" "No, not in the slightest degree." "Was it not a good sermon?" Again came the first answer, "What he *said* was very good." "What do you mean? Why did you not profit by the sermon if what the preacher said was very good?" This was the explanation that the listener gave, "I did not profit by the discourse because I did not believe in the man who delivered it; he was simply an actor performing a part; I did not believe that he felt what he preached, nor that he cared whether we felt or believed it or not."

Where such a state of things as that exists, the hearers cannot be expected to profit by the sermon, no matter what the preacher may say; they may try to fancy that the truths he utters are precious, they may resolve that they will feed upon the provision whoever may set the dish before them; but it is no use, they cannot do it, they cannot separate the heartless speaker from the message he delivers so carelessly. As soon as a man lets his work become a matter of mere form or routine, it sinks into a performance in which the preacher is simply an actor. He is only acting a part, as he might in a play at the theater; and not speaking from his inmost soul, as a man sent from God.

I do beseech you, brethren, speak from your hearts, or else do not speak at all. If you can be silent, be silent; but if you must speak for God, be thoroughly sincere about it. It would be better for you to go back to business, and weigh butter or sell reels of cotton, or do anything rather than pretend to be ministers of the gospel unless God has called you to the work. I believe that the most damnable thing a man can do is to preach the gospel merely as an actor, and to turn the worship of God into a kind of theatrical performance. Such a caricature is more worthy of the devil than of God. Divine truth is far too precious to be made the subject of such a mockery. You may depend upon it that, when the people once suspect that you are insincere, they will never listen to you except with disgust, and they will not be at all likely to believe your message if you give them cause to think that you do not believe it yourselves.

## Earnestness

I hope I am not wrong in supposing that all of us are thoroughly sincere in our Master's service; so I will go on to what seems to me to be the next qualification, manward, for soul-winning, and that is, *evident earnestness*. The command to the man who would be a true servant of the Lord Jesus Christ is, "Thou shalt love the Lord thy

God with all thy heart, and with all thy soul, and with all thy strength, and with all thy mind." If a man is to be a soul-winner, there must be in him intensity of emotion as well as sincerity of heart. You may preach the most solemn warnings, and the most dreadful threatenings, in such an indifferent or careless way that no one will be in the least affected by them; and you may repeat the most affectionate exhortations in such a half-hearted manner that no one will be moved either to love or fear.

I believe, brethren, that for soul-winning there is more in this matter of earnestness than in almost anything else. I have seen and heard some who were very poor preachers, who yet brought many souls to the Savior through the earnestness with which they delivered their message. There was positively nothing in their sermons (until the provision merchant used them to wrap round his butter), yet those feeble sermons brought many to Christ. It was not what the preachers said, so much as how they said it, that carried conviction to the hearts of their hearers. The simplest truth was so driven home by the intensity of the utterance and emotion of the man from whom it came that it told with surprising effect. If any gentleman here would present me with a cannon-ball, say one weighing fifty or a hundred pounds, and let me roll it across the room; and another would entrust me with a rifle-ball, and a rifle out of which I could fire it, I know which would be the more effective of the two. Let no man despise the little bullet, for very often that is the one that kills the sin, and kills the sinner, too.

So, brethren, it is not the bigness of the words you utter; it is the force with which you deliver them that decides what is to come of the utterance. I have heard of a ship that was fired at by the cannon in a fort, but no impression was made upon it until the general in command gave the order for the balls to be made red-hot, and then the vessel was sent to the bottom of the sea in three minutes. That is what you must do with your sermons, make them red-hot; never mind if men do say you are too enthusiastic, or even too fanatical, give them red-hot shot, there is nothing else half as good for the purpose you have in view. We do not go out snow-balling on Sundays, we go fire-balling; we ought to hurl grenades into the enemy's ranks.

What earnestness our theme deserves! We have to tell of an earnest Savior, an earnest heaven, and an earnest hell. How earnest we ought to be when we remember that in our work we have to deal with souls that are immortal, with sin that is eternal in its effects, with pardon that is infinite, and with terrors and joys that are to last for ever and ever! A man who is not in earnest when he has such a theme as this,—can he possess a heart at all? Could one be discovered even with a microscope? If he were dissected, probably all that could be found would be a pebble, a heart of stone, or some other substance equally incapable of emotion. I trust that, when God gave us hearts of flesh for ourselves, He gave us hearts that could feel for other people also.

## Love for Those Who Hear

These things being taken for granted, I should say, next, that it is necessary for a man who is to be a soul-winner, that he should have an *evident love to his hearers*. I cannot imagine a man being a winner of souls when he spends most of his time in abusing his congregation, and talking as if he hated the very sight of them. Such men seem happy only when they are emptying vials of wrath over those who have the unhappiness of listening to them. I heard of a brother preaching from the text, "A certain man went down from Jerusalem to Jericho, and fell among thieves." He began his discourse thus, "I do not say that this man came to the place where we are, but I do know another man who did come to this place, and fell among thieves." You can easily guess what would be the result of such vitriol-throwing. I know of one who preached from the passage, "And Aaron held his peace," and one who heard him said that the difference between him and Aaron was, that Aaron held his peace, and the preacher did not; but, on the contrary, he raved at the people with all his might.

You must have a real desire for the good of the people if you are to have much influence over them. Why, even dogs and cats love the people who love them, and human beings are much the same as these dumb animals. People very soon get to know when a cold man gets into the pulpit, one of those who seem to have been carved out of a block of marble. There have been one or two of our brethren of that kind, and they have never succeeded anywhere. When I have asked the cause of their failure, in each case the reply has been, "He is a good man, a very good man; he preaches well, very well, but still we do not get on with him." I have asked, "Why do you not like him?" The reply has been, "Nobody ever did like him." "Is he quarrelsome?" "Oh! dear no, I wish he would make a row." I try to fish out what the drawback is, for I am very anxious to know, and at last someone says, "Well, sir, I do not think he has any heart; at least, he does not preach and act as if he had any."

It is very sad when the failure of any ministry is caused by want of heart. You ought to have a great big heart, like the harbor at Portsmouth or Plymouth, so that all the people in your congregation could come and cast anchor in it, and feel that they were under the lee of a great rock. Do you not notice that men succeed in the ministry, and win souls for Christ, just in proportion as they are men with large hearts? Think, for instance, of Dr. Brock; there was a mass of a man, one who had bowels of compassion; and what is the good of a minister who has not? I do not hold up the accumulation of flesh as an object worthy of your attainment; but I do say that you must have big hearts, if you are to win men to Jesus; you must be Greathearts if you are to lead many pilgrims to the Celestial City.

I have seen some very lean men who said that they were perfectly holy, and I could almost believe that they could not sin, for they were like old bits of leather, there did not appear to be anything in them that was capable of sinning. I met one of these "perfect" brethren once, and he was just like a piece of sea-weed, there was no humanity in him. I like to see a trace of humanity somewhere or other about a man, and people in general like it, too; they get on better with a man who has some human nature in him. Human nature, in some aspects, is an awful thing; but when the Lord Jesus Christ took it, and joined His own divine nature to it, He made a grand thing of it, and human nature is a noble thing when it is united to the Lord Jesus Christ.

Those men who keep themselves to themselves, like hermits, and live a supposed sanctified life of self-absorption, are not likely to have any influence in the world, or to do good to their fellow-creatures. You must love the people, and mix with them, if you are to be of service to them. There are some ministers who really are much better men than others, yet they do not accomplish so much good as those who are more human, those who go and sit down with the people, and make themselves as much as possible at home with them. You know, brethren, that it is possible for you to appear to be just a wee bit too good, so that people will feel that you are altogether transcendental beings, and fitter to preach to angels, and cherubim, and seraphim, than to the fallen sons of Adam.

Just be men among men; keeping yourselves clear of all their faults and vices, but mingling with them in perfect love and sympathy, and feeling that you would do anything in your power to bring them to Christ, so that you might even say with the apostle Paul, "Though I be free from all men, yet have I made myself servant unto all, that I might gain the more. And unto the Jews I became as a Jew, that I might gain the Jews; to them that are under the law, as under the law, that I might gain them that are under the law; to them that are without law, as without law (being not without law to God, but under the law to Christ), that I might gain them that are without law. To the weak became I as weak, that I might gain the weak: I am made all things to all men, that I might by all means save some."

## Unselfishness

The next qualification, manward, for soul-winning is *evident unselfishness*. A man ceases to bring men to Christ as soon as he becomes known as a selfish man. Selfishness seems to be ingrained in some people; you see it at the table at home, in the house of God, everywhere. When such individuals come to deal with a church and congregation, their selfishness soon manifests itself; they mean to get all they can, although in the Baptist ministry they do not often get much.

I hope each of you, brethren, will be willing to say,

"Well, let me have but food and raiment, and I will be therewith content." If you try to put the thought of money altogether away from you, the money will often come back to you doubled; but if you seek to grab and grasp all, you will very likely find that it will not come to you at all. Those who are selfish in the matter of salary, will be the same in everything else; they will not want their people to know anybody who can preach better than themselves; and they cannot bear to hear of any good work going on anywhere except in their own chapel. If there is a revival at another place, and souls are being saved, they say, with a sneer, "Oh! yes, there are many converts, but what are they? Where will they be in a few months' time?" They think far more of their own gain of one new member per year than of their neighbor's hundreds at one time.

If your people see that kind of selfishness in you, you will soon lose power over them; if you make up your mind that you will be a great man, whoever has to be thrust on one side, you will go to the cats as sure as you are alive. What are you, my dear brother, that people should all bow down and worship you, and think that in all the world there is none beside you? I tell you what it is; the less you think of yourself, the more will people think of you; and the more you think of yourself, the less will people think of you. If any of you have any trace of selfishness about you, pray get rid of it at once, or you will never be fit instruments for the winning of souls for the Lord Jesus Christ.

## Holiness

Then I am sure that another thing that is wanted in a

soul-winner is *holiness of character*. It is no use talking about "the higher life" on Sundays, and then living the lower life on week days. A Christian minister must be very careful, not only to be innocent of actual wrong-doing, but not to be a cause of offence to the weak ones of the flock. All things are lawful, but all things are not expedient. We ought never to do anything that we judge to be wrong, but we ought also to be willing to abstain from things which might not be wrong in themselves, but which might be an occasion of stumbling to others. When people see that we not only preach about holiness, but that we are ourselves holy men, they will be drawn towards holy things by our character as well as by our preaching.

## Seriousness

I think also that, if we are to be soul-winners, there must be about us *a seriousness of manner*. Some brethren are serious by nature. There was a gentleman in a railway carriage, some time ago, who overheard a conversation between two of the passengers. One of them said, "Well, now, I think the church of Rome has great power, and is likely to succeed with the people, because of the evident holiness of her ministers. There is, for instance, Cardinal _____, he is just like a skeleton; through his long fasting and prayers, he has reduced himself almost to skin and bone. Whenever I hear him speak, I feel at once the force of the holiness of the man. Now, look at Spurgeon, he eats and drinks like an ordinary mortal; I would not give a pin to hear him preach." His friend heard him very patiently, and then said quite quietly, "Did it ever strike you that the Cardinal's appearance was to be accounted for by the fact of his liver being out of order? I do not think it is grace that makes him as lean as he is, I believe it is his liver."

So, there are some brethren who are naturally of a melancholy disposition, they are always very serious; but in them it is not a sign of grace, it is only an indication that their livers are out of order. They never laugh, they think it would be wicked to do so; but they go about the world increasing the misery of human kind, which is dreadful enough without the addition of their unnecessary portion. Such people evidently imagine that they were predestinated to pour buckets of cold water upon all human mirth and joy. So, dear brethren, if any of you are very serious, you must not always attribute it to grace, for it may be all owing to the state of your liver.

The most of us, however, are far more inclined to that laughter which doeth good like medicine, and we shall need all our cheerfulness, if we are to comfort and lift up those who are cast down; but we shall never bring many souls to Christ, if we are full of that levity which characterizes some men. People will say, "It is all a joke; just hear how those young fellows jest about religion, it is one thing to listen to them when they are in the pulpit, but it quite another matter to listen to them when they are sitting round the supper table."

I have heard of a man who was dying, and he sent for the minister to come and see him. When the minister came in, the dying man said to him, "Do you remember a young man walking with you one evening, some years ago, when you were going out to preach?" He said, he did not. "I recollect it very well," replied the other. "Do you not remember preaching at such-and-such a village, from such-and-such a text, and after the service a young man walked home with you?" "Oh, yes, I remember that very well!" "Well, I am the young man who walked home with you that night; I remember your sermon, I shall never forget it." "Thank God for that," said the preacher. "No," answered the dying man, "you will not thank God when you have heard all I have to say. I walked with you to the village, but you did not say much to me on the way there, for you were thinking over your sermon; you deeply impressed me while you were preaching, and I was led to think about giving my heart to Christ. I wanted to speak to you about my soul on the way home; but the moment you got out you cracked a joke, and all the way back you made such fun upon serious subjects, that I could not say anything about what I felt, and it thoroughly disgusted me with religion, and all who professed it, and now I am going to be damned, and my blood will lie at your door, as sure as you are alive:" and so he passed out of the world. One would not like anything of that sort to happen to himself; therefore, take heed, brethren, that you give no occasion for it. There must be a prevailing seriousness about our whole lives, otherwise we cannot hope to lead other men to Christ.

## Tenderness

Finally, if we are to be much used of God as soul-winners, there must be in our hearts *a great deal of tenderness*. I like a man to have a due amount of holy boldness, but I do not care to see him brazenfaced and impudent. A young man goes into a pulpit, apologizes for attempting to preach, and hopes the people will bear with him; he does not know that he has anything particular to say, if the Lord had sent him he might have had some message for them, but he feels himself so young and inexperienced that he cannot speak very positively about anything. Such talk as that will never save a mouse, much less an immortal soul. If the Lord has sent you to preach the gospel, why should you make any apologies? Ambassadors do not apologize when they go to a foreign court; they know that their monarch has sent them, and they deliver their message with all the authority of king and country at their back.

Nor is it worth while for you to call attention to your youth. You are only a trumpet of ram's horn; and it does not matter whether you were pulled off the ram's head yesterday, or five-and-twenty years ago. If God blows through you, there will be noise enough, and something more than noise; if He does not, nothing will come of the blowing. When you preach, speak out straight, but be very tender about it; and if there is an unpleasant thing to be said, take care that you put it in the kindest possible form.

Some of our brethren had a message to deliver to a certain Christian brother, and when they went to him they put it so awkwardly that he was grievously offended. When I spoke to him about the same matter, he said, "I would not have minded your speaking to me; you have a way of putting an unpleasant truth so that a man cannot be offended with you however much he may dislike the message you bring to him." "Well, but," I said, "I put the matter just as strongly as the other brethren did." "Yes, you did," he replied, "but they said it in such a nasty kind of a way that I would not stand it. Why, sir, I had rather be blown up by you than praised by those other people!"

There is a way of doing such things so that the person reproved feels positively grateful to you. One may kick a man downstairs in such a fashion that he will rather like it; while another may open a door in such an offensive way that you do not want to go through till he is out of the way. Now, if I have to tell anyone certain unpalatable truths which it is necessary that he should know if his soul is to be saved, it is a stern necessity for me to be faithful to him; yet I will try so to deliver my message that he shall not be offended at it. Then, if he does take offense, he must; the probability is that he will not, but that what I say will take effect upon his conscience.

I know some brethren who preach as if they were prize-fighters. When they are in the pulpit, they remind me of the Irishman at Donnybrook Fair; all the way through the sermon they appear to be calling upon someone to come up and fight them, and they are never happy except when they are pitching into somebody or other. There is a man who often preaches on Clapham Common, and he does it so pugnaciously that the infidels whom he assails cannot endure it, and there are frequent fights and rows. There is a way of preaching so as to set everybody by the ears; if some men were allowed to preach in heaven, I am afraid they would set the angels fighting. I know a number of ministers of this stamp.

There is one who, to my certain knowledge, has been at over a dozen places during his not very long ministerial life. You can tell where he has been by the ruin he leaves behind him. He always finds the churches in a sad state, and he straightway begins to purify them, that is, to destroy them. As a general rule, the first thing, out goes the principal deacon, and the next, away go all the leading families, and before long, the man has purified the place so effectively that the few people who are left cannot keep him. Off he goes to another place, and repeats the process of destruction. He is a kind of spiritual ship-scuttler, and he is never happy except when he is boring a hole through the planks of some good vessel. He says he believes the ship is unsound; so he bores, and bores, until just as she is going down, he slips off, and gets aboard another vessel, which very soon sinks in the same manner. He feels that he is called to the work of separating the precious from the vile, and a preciously vile mess he makes of it. I have no reason to believe it is the condition of the liver in this brother, it is more likely that there is something wrong with his heart; certainly, there is an evil disease upon him that always makes me get into a bad temper with him. It is dangerous to entertain him above three days, for he would quarrel in that time with the most peaceably disposed man in the world. I never mean to recommend him to a pastorate again; let him find a place for himself if he can, for I believe that, wherever he goes, the place will be like the spot where the foot of the Tartar's horse is put down, the grass will never again grow there.

If any of you brethren have even a little of this nasty, bitter spirit about you, go to sea that you may get rid of it. I hope it may happen to you according to the legend which is told concerning Mahomet. "In every human being," so the story runs, "there are two black drops of sin. The great prophet himself was not free from the common lot of evil; but an angel was sent to take his heart, and squeeze out of it the two black drops of sin." Get those black drops out somehow while you are in college; if you have any malice, or ill-will, or bad temper in you, pray the Lord to take it out of you while you are here; do not go into the churches to fight as others have done.

"Still," says a brother, "I am not going to let the people tread on me. I shall take the bull by the horns." You will be a great fool if you do. I never felt that I was called to do anything of the kind. Why not let the bull alone, to go where he likes? A bull is a very likely creature to project you into space if you get meddling with his horns. "Still," says another, "we must set things right." Yes, but the best way to set things right is not to make them more wrong than they are. Nobody thinks of putting a mad bull into a china shop in order to get the china cleaned, and no one can by a display of evil temper set right anything that is wrong in our churches. Take care always to speak the truth in love, and especially when you are rebuking sin.

I believe, brethren, that soul-winning is to be done by men of the character I have been describing; and most of all will this be the case when they are surrounded by people of a similar character. You want to get the very atmosphere in which you live and labor permeated with this spirit before you can rightly expect the fullest and richest blessings. Therefore, may you and all your people be all that I have pictured, for the Lord Jesus Christ's sake! Amen.

*Spurgeon's 1875 work,* Lectures to My Students, *continues to be a valuable aid to pastors. Though "The Preacher's Private Prayer" is intended for an audience of pastors, Spurgeon's advice is applicable to all men of prayer, such as Spurgeon himself was. He finds that constant prayer is a necessity in the lives of pastors and will incomparably assist them in their work, advice that is true for all those who pray.*

〜

## CHAPTER NINE

---

# *The Preacher's Private Prayer*

Of course the preacher is above all others distinguished as a man of prayer. He prays as an ordinary Christian, else he were a hypocrite. He prays more than ordinary Christians, else he were disqualified for the office which he has undertaken. "It would be wholly monstrous," says Bernard, "for a man to be highest in office and lowest in soul; first in station and last in life." Over all his other relationships the pre-eminence of the pastor's responsibility casts a halo, and if true to his Master, he becomes distinguished for his prayerfulness in them all. As a citizen, his country has the advantage of his intercession; as a neighbor those under his shadow are remembered in supplication. He prays as a husband and as a father; he strives to make his family devotions a model for his flock; and if the fire on the altar of God should burn low anywhere else, it is well tended in the house of the Lord's chosen servant—for he takes care that the morning and evening sacrifice shall sanctify his dwelling. But there are some of his prayers which concern his office, and of those our plan in these lectures leads us to speak most. He offers peculiar supplications *as a minister*, and he draws near to God in this respect, over and above all his approaches in his other relationships.

## Incessant Prayer

I take it that as a minister *he is always praying*. Whenever his mind turns to his work, whether he is in it or out of it, he ejaculates a petition, sending up his holy desires as well-directed arrows to the skies. He is not always in the act of prayer, but he lives in the spirit of it. If his heart be in his work, he cannot eat or drink, or take recreation, or go to his bed, or rise in the morning, without evermore feeling a fervency of desire, a weight of anxiety, and a simplicity of dependence upon God; thus, in one form or other he continues in prayer. If there be any man under heaven, who is compelled to carry out the precept—"Pray without ceasing," surely it is the Christian minister. He has peculiar temptations, special trials, singular difficulties, and remarkable duties, he has to deal with God in awful relationships, and with men in mysterious interests; he therefore needs much more grace than common men, and as he knows this, he is led constantly to cry to the strong for strength, and say, "I will lift up mine eyes unto the hills, from whence cometh my help."

Alleine once wrote to a dear friend, "Though I am apt to be unsettled and quickly set off the hinges, yet, methinks, I am like a bird out of the nest, I am never quiet till I am in my old way of communion with God; like the needle in the compass, that is restless till it be turned towards the pole. I can say, through grace, with the church, 'With my soul have I desired thee in the night, and with my spirit within me have I sought thee early.' My heart is early and late with God; 'tis the business and delight of my life to seek him.'' Such must be the even tenor of your way, O men of God. If you as ministers are not very prayerful, you are much to be pitied. If, in the future, you shall be called to sustain pastorates, large or small, if you become lax in secret devotion, not only will *you* need to be pitied, but your people also; and, in addition to that, you shall be blamed, and the day cometh in which you shall be ashamed and confounded.

It may scarcely be needful to commend to you the sweet uses of private devotion, and yet I cannot forbear. To you, as the ambassadors of God, the mercy-seat has a virtue beyond all estimate; the more familiar you are with the court of heaven the better shall you discharge your heavenly trust. Among all the formative influences which go to make up a man honoured of God in the ministry, I know of none more mighty than his own familiarity with the mercy-seat. All that a college course can do for a student is coarse and external compared with the spiritual and delicate refinement obtained by communion with God. While the unformed minister is revolving upon the wheel of preparation, prayer is the tool of the great potter by which he molds the vessel. All our libraries and studies are mere emptiness compared with our closets. We grow, we wax mighty, we prevail in private prayer.

## Prayer Aids in Preparation

Your prayers will be your ablest assistants *while your discourses are yet upon the anvil*. While other men, like

Esau, are hunting for their portion, you, by the aid of prayer, will find the savory meat near at home, and may say in truth what Jacob said so falsely, "The Lord brought it to me." If you can dip your pens into your hearts, appealing in earnestness to the Lord, you will write well; and if you can gather your matter on your knees at the gate of heaven, you will not fail to speak well. Prayer, as a mental exercise, will bring many subjects before the mind, and so help in the selection of a topic, while as a high spiritual engagement it will cleanse your inner eye that you may see truth in the light of God. Texts will often refuse to reveal their treasures till you open them with the key of prayer. How wonderfully were the books opened to Daniel when he was in supplication! How much Peter learned upon the housetop!

The closet is the best study. The commentators are good instructors, but the Author himself is far better, and prayer makes a direct appeal to him and enlists him in our cause. It is a great thing to pray one's self into the spirit and marrow of a text; working into it by sacred feeding thereon, even as the worm bores its way into the kernal of the nut. Prayer supplies a leverage for the uplifting of ponderous truths. One marvels how the stones of Stonehenge could have been set in their places; it is even more to be enquired after whence some men obtained such admirable knowledge of mysterious doctrines: was not prayer the potent machinery which wrought the wonder? Waiting upon God often turns darkness into light. Persevering enquiry at the sacred oracle uplifts the veil and gives grace to look into the deep things of God. A certain Puritan divine at a debate was observed frequently to write upon the paper before him; upon others curiously seeking to read his notes, they found nothing upon the page but the words, "More light, Lord," "More light, Lord," repeated scores of times: a most suitable prayer for the student of the Word when preparing his discourse.

You will frequently find fresh streams of thought leaping up from the passage before you, as if the rock had been struck by Moses' rod; new veins of precious ore will be revealed to your astonished gaze as you quarry God's Word and use diligently the hammer of prayer. You will sometimes feel as if you were entirely shut up, and then suddenly a new road will open before you. He who hath the key of David openeth, and no man shutteth. If you have ever sailed down the Rhine, the water scenery of that majestic river will have struck you as being very like in effect to a series of lakes. Before and behind the vessel appears to be enclosed in massive walls of rock, or circles of vine-clad terraces, till on a sudden you turn a corner, and before you the rejoicing and abounding river flows onward in its strength. So the laborious student often finds it with a text; it appears to be fast closed against you, but prayer propels your vessel, and turns its prow into fresh waters, and you behold the broad and deep stream of sacred truth flowing in its fulness, and bearing you with it. Is not this a convincing reason for abiding in supplication? Use prayer as a boring rod, and wells of living water will leap up from the bowels of the Word. Who will be content to thirst when living waters are so readily to be obtained!

The best and holiest men have ever made prayer the most important part of pulpit preparation. It is said of McCheyne, "Anxious to give his people on the Sabbath what had cost him somewhat, he never, without an urgent reason, went before them without much previous meditation and prayer. His principle on this subject was embodied in a remark he made to some of us who were conversing on the matter. Being asked his view of diligent preparation for the pulpit, he reminded us of Exodus 27:20. *'Beaten oil—beaten oil for the lamps of the sanctuary.'* And yet his prayerfulness was greater still. Indeed, he could not neglect fellowship with God before entering the congregation. He needed to be bathed in the love of God. His ministry was so much a bringing out of views that had first sanctified his own soul, that the healthiness of his soul was absolutely needful to the vigor and power of his ministrations.'' "With him the commencement of all labor invariably consisted in the preparation of his own soul. The walls of his chamber were witnesses of his prayerfulness and of his tears, as well as of his cries."

## Prayer Assists in Delivery

*Prayer will singularly assist you in the delivery of your sermon;* in fact, nothing can so gloriously fit you to preach as descending fresh from the mount of communion with God to speak with men. None are so able to plead with men as those who have been wrestling with God on their behalf. It is said of Alleine, "He poured out his very heart in prayer and preaching. His supplications and his exhortations were so affectionate, so full of holy zeal, life and vigor, that they quite overcame his hearers; he melted over them, so that he thawed and mollified, and sometimes dissolved the hardest hearts." There could have been none of this sacred dissolving of heart if his mind had not been previously exposed to the tropical rays of the Sun of Righteousness by private fellowship with the risen Lord. A truly pathetic delivery, in which there is no affectation, but much affection, can only be the offspring of prayer. There is no rhetoric like that of the heart, and no school for learning it but the foot of the cross. It were better that you never learned a rule of human oratory, but were full of the power of heavenborn love, than that you should master Quintilian, Cicero, and Aristotle, and remain without the apostolic anointing.

Prayer may not make you eloquent after the human mode, but it will make you truly so, for you will speak out of the heart; and is not that the meaning of the word eloquence? It will bring fire from heaven upon your sacrifice, and thus prove it to be accepted of the Lord.

As fresh springs of thought will frequently break up during preparation in answer to prayer, so will it be in the delivery of the sermon. Most preachers who depend upon God's Spirit will tell you that their freshest and best thoughts are not those which were premeditated, but ideas which come to them, flying as on the wings of angels; unexpected treasures brought on a sudden by celestial hands, seeds of the flowers of paradise, wafted from the mountains of myrrh. Often and often when I have felt hampered, both in thought and expression, my secret groaning of heart has brought me relief, and I have enjoyed more than usual liberty. But how dare we pray in the battle if we have never cried to the Lord while buckling on the harness! The remembrance of his wrestlings at home comforts the fettered preacher when in the pulpit: God will not desert us unless we have deserted him. You, brethren, will find that prayer will ensure you strength equal to your day.

As the tongues of fire came upon the apostles, when they sat watching and praying, even so will they come upon you. You will find yourselves, when you might perhaps have flagged, suddenly upborne, as by a seraph's power. Wheels of fire will be fastened to your chariot, which had begun to drag right heavily, and steeds angelic will be in a moment harnessed to your fiery car, till you climb the heavens like Elijah, in a rapture of flaming inspiration.

## Prayer after the Sermon

*After the sermon,* how would a conscientious preacher give vent to his feelings and find solace for his soul if access to the mercy-seat were denied him? Elevated to the highest pitch of excitement, how can we relieve our souls but in importunate pleadings. Or depressed by a fear of failure, how shall we be comforted but in moaning out our complaint before our God. How often have some of us tossed to and fro upon our couch half the night because of conscious shortcomings in our testimony! How frequently have we longed to rush back to the pulpit again to say over again more vehemently, what we have uttered in so cold a manner! Where could we find rest for our spirits but in confession of sin, and passionate entreaty that our infirmity or folly might in no way hinder the Spirit of God!

It is not possible in a public assembly to pour out all our heart's love to our flock. Like Joseph, the affectionate minister will seek where to weep; his emotions, however freely he may express himself, will be pent up in the pulpit, and only in private prayer can he draw up the sluices and bid them flow forth. If we cannot prevail with men for God, we will, at least, endeavor to prevail with God for men. We cannot save them, or even persuade them to be saved, but we can at least bewail their madness and entreat the interference of the Lord. Like Jeremiah, we can make it our resolve, "If ye will not hear it, my soul shall weep in secret places for your pride, and mine eye shall weep sore and run down with tears." To such pathetic appeals the Lord's heart can never be indifferent; in due time the weeping intercessor will become the rejoicing winner of souls.

There is a distinct connection between importunate agonizing and true success, even as between the travail and the birth, the sowing in tears and the reaping in joy. "How is it that your seed comes up so soon?" said one gardener to another. "Because I steep it," was the reply. We must steep all our teachings in tears, "when none but God is nigh," and their growth will surprise and delight us. Could any one wonder at Brainerd's success, when his diary contains such notes as this: "Lord's Day, April 25th—This morning spent about two hours in sacred duties, and was enabled, more than ordinarily, to agonize for immortal souls; though it was early in the morning, and the sun scarcely shone at all, yet my body was quite wet with sweat." The secret of Luther's power lay in the same direction. Theodorus said of him: "I overheard him in prayer, but, good God, with what life and spirit did he pray! It was with so much reverence, as if he were speaking to God, yet with so much confidence as if he were speaking to his friend."

My brethren, let me beseech you to be men of prayer. Great talents you may never have, but you will do well enough without them if you abound in intercession. If you do not pray over what you have sown, God's sovereignty may possibly determine to give a blessing, but you have no right to expect it, and if it comes it will bring no comfort to your own heart. I was reading yesterday a book by Father Faber, late of the Oratory, at Brompton, a marvellous compound of truth and error. In it he relates a legend to this effect. A certain preacher, whose sermons converted men by scores, received a revelation from heaven that not one of the conversions was owing to his talents or eloquence, but all to the prayers of an illiterate lay-brother, who sat on the pulpit steps, pleading all the time for the success of the sermon. It may in the all-revealing day be so with us. We may discover, after having labored long and wearily in preaching, that all the honor belongs to another builder, whose prayers were gold, silver, and precious stones, while our sermonizings being apart from prayer, were but hay and stubble.

## Prayer Throughout the Ministry

When we have done with preaching, we shall not, if we are true ministers of God, have done with praying, because the whole church, with many tongues, will be crying, in the language of the Macedonian, "Come over and help us" in prayer. If you are enabled to prevail in prayer you will have many requests to offer for others who will flock to you, and beg a share in your intercessions, and so you will find yourselves commissioned with errands to the mercy-seat for friends and hearers.

Such is always my lot, and I feel it a pleasure to have such requests to present before my Lord. Never can you be short of themes for prayer, even if no one should suggest them to you. Look at your congregation. There are always sick folk among them, and many more who are soul-sick. Some are unsaved, others are seeking and cannot find. Many are desponding, and not a few believers are backsliding or mourning. There are widows' tears and orphans' sighs to be put into our bottle, and poured out before the Lord. If you are a genuine minister of God you will stand as a priest before the Lord, spiritually wearing the ephod and the breast-plate whereon you bear the names of the children of Israel, pleading for them within the veil. I have known brethren who have kept a list of persons for whom they felt bound especially to pray, and I doubt not such a record often reminded them of what might otherwise have slipped their memory.

Nor will your people wholly engross you; the nation and the world will claim their share. The man who is mighty in prayer may be a wall of fire around his country, her guardian angel and her shield. We have all heard how the enemies of the Protestant cause dreaded the prayers of Knox more than they feared armies of ten thousand men. The famous Welch was also a great intercessor for his country; he used to say, "he wondered how a Christian could lie in his bed all night and not rise to pray." When his wife, fearing that he would take cold, followed him into the room to which he had withdrawn, she heard him pleading in broken sentences, "Lord, wilt thou not grant me Scotland?" O that we were thus wrestling at midnight, crying, "Lord, wilt thou not grant us our hearers' souls?"

The minister who does not earnestly pray over his work must surely be a vain and conceited man. He acts as if he thought himself sufficient of himself, and therefore needed not to appeal to God. Yet what a baseless pride to conceive that our preaching can ever be in itself so powerful that it can turn men from their sins, and bring them to God without the working of the Holy Ghost. If we are truly humble-minded we shall not venture down to the fight until the Lord of Hosts has clothed us with all power, and said to us, "Go in this thy might."

The preacher who neglects to pray much must be very careless about his ministry. He cannot have comprehended his calling. He cannot have computed the value of a soul, or estimated the meaning of eternity. He must be a mere official, tempted into a pulpit because the piece of bread which belongs to the priest's office is very necessary to him, or a detestable hypocrite who loves the praise of men, and cares not for the praise of God. He will surely become a mere superficial talker, best approved where grace is least valued and a vain show most admired. He cannot be one of those who plough deep and reap abundant harvests. He is a mere loiterer, not a laborer. As a preacher he has a name to live and is dead. He limps in his life like the lame man in the Proverbs, whose legs were not equal, for his praying is shorter than his preaching.

I am afraid that, more or less, most of us need self-examination as to this matter. If any man here should venture to say that he prays as much as he ought, as a student, I should gravely question his statement; and if there be a minister, deacon, or elder present who can say that he believes he is occupied with God in prayer to the full extent to which he might be, I should be pleased to know him. I can only say, that if he can claim this excellence, he leaves me far behind, for I can make no such claim: I wish I could; and I make the confession with no small degree of shame-facedness and confusion, but I am obliged to make it. If we are not more negligent than others, this is no consolation to us; the shortcomings of others are no excuses for us.

How few of us could compare ourselves with Mr. Joseph Alleine, whose character I have mentioned before? "At the time of his health," writes his wife, "he did rise constantly at or before four of the clock, and would be much troubled if he heard smiths or other craftsmen at their trades before he was at communion with God; saying to me often, 'How this noise shames me. Does not my

Master deserve more than theirs?' From four till eight he spent in prayer, holy contemplation, and singing of psalms, in which he much delighted and did daily practise alone, as well as in the family. Sometimes he would suspend the routine of parochial engagements, and devote whole days to these secret exercises, in order to which, he would contrive to be alone in some void house, or else in some sequestered spot in the open valley. Here there would be much prayer and meditation on God and heaven."

Could we read Jonathan Edwards' description of David Brainerd and not blush? "His life," says Edwards, "shows the right way to success in the words of the ministry. He sought it as a resolute soldier seeks victory in a siege or battle; or as a man that runs a race for a great prize. Animated with love to Christ and souls, how did he labor always fervently, not only in word and doctrine, in public and private, but in *prayers* day and night, 'wrestling with God' in secret, and 'travailing in birth,' with unutterable groans and agonies! 'until Christ were formed' in the hearts of the people to whom he was sent! How did he thirst for a blessing upon his ministry, 'and watch for souls as one that must give account!' How did he 'go forth in the strength of the Lord God, seeking and depending on the special influence of the Spirit to assist and succeed him! And what was the happy fruit at last, after long waiting and many dark and discouraging appearances: like a true son of Jacob, he persevered in wrestling through all the darkness of the night, until the breaking of the day."

Might not Henry Martyn's journal shame us, where we find such entries as these; "Sept. 24th—The determination with which I went to bed last night, of devoting this day to prayer and fasting, I was enabled to put into execution. In my first prayer for deliverance from worldly thoughts, depending on the power and promises of God, for fixing my soul while I prayed, I was helped to enjoy much abstinence from the world for nearly an hour. Then read the history of Abraham, to see how familiarly God had revealed himself to mortal men of old. Afterwards, in prayer for my own sanctification, my soul breathed freely and ardently after the holiness of God, and this was the best season of the day." We might perhaps more truly join with him in his lament after the first year of his ministry that "he judged he had dedicated too much time to public ministrations, and too little to private communion with God."

## The Blessings of Private Prayer

How much of blessing we may have missed through remissness in supplication we can scarcely guess, and none of us can know how poor we are in comparison with what we might have been if we had lived habitually nearer to God in prayer. Vain regrets and surmises are useless, but an earnest determination to amend will be far more useful. We not only ought to pray more, but we *must*. The fact is, the secret of all ministerial success lies in prevalence at the mercy-seat.

One bright benison which private prayer brings down upon the ministry is an indescribable and inimitable something, better understood than named; it is a dew from the Lord, a divine presence which you will recognize at once when I say it is "an unction from the Holy One." What is it? I wonder how long we might beat our brains before we could plainly put into words what is meant by *preaching with unction;* yet he who preaches knows its presence, and he who hears soon detects its absence; Samaria, in famine, typifies a discourse without it; Jerusalem, with her feasts of fat things full of marrow, may represent a sermon enriched with it. Every one knows what the freshness of the morning is when orient pearls abound on every blade of grass, but who can describe it, much less produce it of itself?

Such is the mystery of spiritual anointing; we know, but we cannot tell to others what it is. It is as easy as it is foolish to counterfeit it, as some do who use expressions which are meant to betoken fervent love, but oftener indicate sickly sentimentalism or mere cant. "Dear Lord!" "Sweet Jesus!" "Precious Christ!" are by them poured out wholesale, till one is nauseated. These familiarities may have been not only tolerable, but even beautiful when they first fell from a saint of God, speaking, as it were, out of the excellent glory, but when repeated flippantly they are not only intolerable, but indecent, if not profane.

Some have tried to imitate unction by unnatural tones and whines; by turning up the whites of their eyes, and lifting their hands in a most ridiculous manner. McCheyne's tone and rhythm one hears from Scotchmen continually: we much prefer his spirit to his mannerism; and all mere mannerism without power is as foul carrion of all life bereft, obnoxious, mischievous. Certain brethren aim at inspiration through exertion and loud shouting; but it does not come: some we have known to stop the discourse, and exclaim, "God bless you," and others gesticulate wildly, and drive their fingernails into the palms of their hands as if they were in convulsions of celestial ardour. Bah! The whole thing smells of the green-room and the stage. The getting up of fervor in hearers by the simulation of it in the preacher is a loathsome deceit to be scorned by honest men. "To affect feeling," says Richard Cecil, "is nauseous and soon detected, but to feel is the readiest way to the hearts of others."

Unction is a thing which you cannot manufacture, and its counterfeits are worse than worthless; yet it is in itself priceless, and beyond measure needful if you would edify believers and bring sinners to Jesus. To the secret pleader with God this secret is committed; upon him rests the dew of the Lord, about him is the perfume which makes glad the heart. If the anointing which we bear come not from the Lord of hosts we are deceivers, and since only in prayer can we obtain it, let us continue instant, constant, fervent in supplication. Let your fleece lie on the threshing-floor of supplication till it is wet with the dew of heaven. Go not to minister in the temple till you have washed in the laver. Think not to be a messenger of grace to others till you have seen the God of grace for yourselves, and had the word from his mouth.

Time spent in quiet prostration of soul before the Lord is most invigorating. David "sat before the Lord;" it is a great thing to hold these sacred sittings; the mind being receptive, like an open flower drinking in the sunbeams, or the sensitive photographic plate accepting the image before it. Quietude, which some men cannot abide, because it reveals their inward poverty, is as a palace of cedar to the wise, for along its hallowed courts the King in his beauty deigns to walk.

> Sacred silence! thou that art
> Floodgate of the deeper heart,
> Offspring of a heavenly kind;
> Frost o' the mouth, and thaw o' the mind.

Priceless as the gift of utterance may be, the practice of

silence in some aspects far excels it. Do you think me a Quaker? Well, be it so. Herein I follow George Fox most lovingly; for I am persuaded that we most of us think too much of speech, which after all is but the shell of thought. Quiet contemplation, still worship, unuttered rapture, these are mine when my best jewels are before me. Brethren, rob not your heart of the deep sea joys; miss not the far-down life, by for ever babbling among the broken shells and foaming surges of the shore.

I would seriously recommend to you, when settled in the ministry, the celebration of extraordinary seasons of devotion. If your ordinary prayers do not keep up the freshness and vigor of your souls, and you feel that you are flagging, get alone for a week, or even a month if possible. We have occasional holidays, why not frequent holy days? We hear of our richer brethren finding time for a journey to Jerusalem; could we not spare time for the less difficult and far more profitable journey to the heavenly city? Isaac Ambrose, once pastor at Preston, who wrote that famous book, "Looking unto Jesus," always set apart one month in the year for seclusion in a hut in a wood at Garstang. No wonder that he was so mighty a divine, when he could regularly spend so long a time in the mount with God.

I notice that the Romanists are accustomed to secure what they call "Retreats," where a number of priests will retire for a time into perfect quietude, to spend the whole of the time in fasting and prayer, so as to inflame their souls with ardor. We may learn from our adversaries. It would be a great thing every now and then for a band of truly spiritual brethren to spend a day or two with each other in real burning agony of prayer. Pastors alone could use much more freedom than in a mixed company. Times of humiliation and supplication for the whole church will also benefit us if we enter into them heartily. Our seasons of fasting and prayer at the Tabernacle have been high days indeed; never has heaven-gate stood wider; never have our hearts been nearer the central glory. I look forward to our month of special devotion, as mariners reckon upon reaching land. Even if our public work were laid aside to give us space for special prayer, it might be a great gain to our churches. A voyage to the golden rivers of fellowship and meditation would be well repaid by a freight of sanctified feeling and elevated thought.

Our silence might be better than our voices if our solitude were spent with God. That was a grand action of old Jerome, when he laid all his pressing engagements aside to achieve a purpose to which he felt a call from heaven. He had a large congregation, as large a one as any of us need want; but he said to his people, "Now it is of necessity that the New Testament should be translated, you must find another preacher: the translation must be made; I am bound for the wilderness, and shall not return till my task is finished." Away he went with his manuscripts, and prayed and laboured, and produced a work—the Latin Vulgate—which will last as long as the world stands; on the whole a most wonderful translation of Holy Scripture. As learning and prayerful retirement together could thus produce an immortal work, if we were sometimes to say to our people when we felt moved to do so, "Dear friends, we really must be gone for a little while to refresh our souls in solitude," our profiting would soon be apparent, and if we did not write Latin Vulgates, yet we should do immortal work, such as would abide the fire.

*Though Spurgeon did not like his prayers to be recorded, some, such as "To the King Eternal," have survived and were gathered posthumously. As powerful as his prayers, like his sermons, may be in print, there is no real way to compare them to what they must have sounded like when his own magnificent voice spoke them.*

CHAPTER TEN

*To the King Eternal*

Our God and Father, draw us to Thyself by Thy
Spirit, and may the few minutes that we spend in prayer
be full of the true spirit of supplication. Grant that none
of us with closed eyes may yet be looking abroad over the
fields of vanity, but may our eyes be really shut to everything else now but that which is spiritual and divine.
May we have communion with God in the secret of our
hearts, and find Him to be to us as a little sanctuary.

O Lord, we do not find it easy to get rid of distracting
thoughts, but we pray Thee help us to draw the sword
against them and drive them away, and as when the
birds came down upon his sacrifice Abraham drove
them away, so may we chase away all cares, all thoughts
of pleasure, everything else, whether it be pleasing or
painful, that would keep us away from real fellowship
with the Father and with His Son Jesus Christ.

## Adoration

We would begin with adoration. We worship from our hearts the Three in One, the infinitely glorious Jehovah, the only living and true God. We adore the Father, the Son, and the Holy Ghost, the God of Abraham, of Isaac, and of Jacob. We are not yet ascended to the place where pure spirits behold the face of God, but we shall soon be there, perhaps much sooner than we think, and we would be there in spirit now, casting our crowns upon the glassy sea before the throne of the Infinite Majesty, and ascribing glory and honor, and power and praise, and dominion and might to Him that sitteth upon the throne, and unto the Lamb for ever and ever.

All the church doth worship Thee, O God, every heart renewed by grace takes a delight in adoring Thee, and we, among the rest, though least and meanest of them all, yet would bow as heartily as any worshipping, loving, praising, in our soul, being silent unto God because our joy in Him is altogether inexpressible.

Lord help us to worship Thee in life as well as lip. May our whole being be taken up with Thee. As when the fire fell down on Elijah's sacrifice of old and licked up even the water that was in the trenches, so may the consuming fire of the Divine Spirit use up all our nature, and even that which might seem to hinder, even out of that may God get glory by the removal of it. Thus could we adore.

## We Remember Our Condition

But, oh! dear Savior, we come to Thee, and we remember what our state is, and the condition we are in encourages us to come to Thee now as beggars, as dependents upon Thy heavenly charity. Thou art a Savior, and as such Thou art on the outlook for those that need saving, and here we are, here we come. We are the men and women Thou art looking for, needing a Savior.

Great Physician, we bring Thee our wounds and bruises and putrifying sores, and the more diseased we are and the more conscious we are to-day of the depravity of our nature, of the deep-seated corruption of our hearts, the more we feel that we are the sort of beings that Thou art seeking for, for the whole have no need of a physician but they that are sick.

Glorious Benefactor, we can meet Thee on good terms, for we are full of poverty, we are just as empty as we can be. We could not be more abjectly dependent than we are. Since Thou wouldest display Thy mercy here is our sin; since Thou wouldest show Thy strength here is our weakness; since Thou wouldest manifest Thy lovingkindness here are our needs; since Thou wouldest glorify Thy grace here are we, such persons as can never have a shadow of a hope except through Thy grace, for we are undeserving, ill-deserving, hell-deserving, and if Thou do not magnify Thy grace in us we must perish for ever.

And somehow we feel it sweet to come to Thee in this way. If we had to tell Thee that we had some good thing in us which Thou didst require of us, we should be questioning whether we were not flattering ourselves and presumptuously thinking that we were better than we are. Lord Jesus, we come just as we are; this is how we came at first, and this is how we come still, with all our failures, with all our transgressions, with all and everything that is what it ought not to be we come to Thee. We do bless Thee that Thou dost receive us and our wounds, and by Thy stripes we are healed; Thou dost receive us and our sins, and by Thy sin-bearing we are set clear and free from sin. Thou dost receive us and our death, even our death, for Thou art He that liveth and was dead, and art alive for evermore.

We just come and lie at Thy feet, obedient to that call of Thine, "Come unto Me all ye that labor and I will give you rest." Let us feel sweet rest, since we do come at Thy call. May some come that have never come till this day, and may others who have been coming these many years consciously come again, coming unto Thee as unto a living stone, chosen of God and precious, to build our everlasting hopes upon.

## Supplication

But, Lord, now that we are come so near Thee, and on right terms with Thee, we venture to ask Thee this, that we that love Thee may love Thee very much more. Oh! since Thou hast been precious, Thy very name has music in it to our ears, and there are times when Thy love is so inexpressibly strong upon us that we are carried away with it. We have felt that we would gladly die to increase Thine honor. We have been willing to lose our name and our repute if so be Thou mightest be glorified, and truly we often feel that if the crushing of us would lift Thee one inch the higher, we would gladly suffer it.

For oh! Thou blessed King, we would set the crown on Thy head, even if the sword should smite our arm off at the shoulder blade. Thou must be King whatever becomes of us; Thou must be glorified whatever becomes of us.

But yet we have to mourn that we cannot get always to feel as we should this rapture and ardor of love. Oh! at times Thou dost manifest Thyself to us so charmingly that heaven itself could scarce be happier than the world becomes when Thou art with us in it. But when Thou art gone and we are in the dark, oh! give us the love that loves in the dark, that loves when there is no comfortable sense of Thy presence. Let us not be dependent upon feeling, but may we ever love Thee, so that if Thou didst turn Thy back on us by the year together we would think none the less of Thee, for Thou art unspeakably to be beloved whatsoever Thou doest, and if Thou dost give us rough words, yet still we would cling to Thee, and if the rod be used till we tingle again, yet still will we love Thee, for Thou art infinitely to be beloved of all men and angels, and Thy Father loved Thee. Make our hearts to love Thee evermore the same. With all the capacity for love that there is in us, and with all the more that Thou canst give us, may we love our Lord in spirit and in truth.

Help us, Lord, to conquer sin out of love to Thee. Help some dear strugglers that have been mastered by sin sometimes, and they are struggling against it; give them the victory, Lord, and when the battle gets very sharp, and they are tempted to give way a little, help them to be very firm and very strong, never giving up hope in the Lord Jesus, and resolving that if they perish they will perish at His feet and nowhere else but there.

Lord raise up in our churches many men and women that are all on fire with love to Christ and His divine gospel. Oh! give us back again men like Antipas, Thy faithful martyr, men like Paul, Thy earnest servant who proclaimed Thy truth so boldly. Give us Johns, men to whom the Spirit may speak, who shall bid us hear what the Spirit saith unto the churches. Lord revive us! Lord revive us; revive Thy work in the midst of the years in all the churches. Return unto the Church of God in this country, return unto her. Thine adversaries think to have it all their own way, but they will not, for the Lord liveth, and blessed be our Rock.

Because of truth and righteousness, we beseech Thee lay bare Thine arm in these last days. O Shepherd of Israel, deal a heavy blow at the wolves and keep Thy sheep in their own true pastures, free from the poisonous pastures of error. O God, we would stir Thee up. We know Thou sleepest not, and yet sometimes it seems as if Thou didst sleep awhile and leave things to go on in their own way.

We beseech Thee awake. Plead Thine own cause. We know Thine answer, "Awake! awake! put on thy strength, O Zion." This we would do, Lord, but we cannot do it unless Thou dost put forth Thy strength to turn our weakness into might.

Great God, save this nation! O God of heaven and earth, stay the floods of infidelity and of filthiness that roll over this land. Would God we might see better days! Men seem entirely indifferent now. They will not come to hear the Word as once they did. God of our fathers let Thy Spirit work again among the masses. Turn the hearts of the people to the hearing of the Word, and convert them when they hear it. May it be preached with the Holy Ghost sent down from heaven.

Our hearts are weary for Thee, Thou King, Thou King forgotten in thine own land, Thou King despised among Thine own people, when wilt Thou yet be glorious before the eyes of all mankind? Come, we beseech Thee, come quickly, or if Thou comest not personally, send forth the Holy Spirit with a greater power than ever that our hearts may leap within us as they see miracles of mercy repeated in our midst.

Father, glorify Thy Son. Somehow our prayer always

comes to this before we have done. "Father, glorify Thy Son that Thy Son also may glorify Thee," and let the days come when He shall see of the travail of His soul and shall be satisfied. Bless all work done for Thee, whether it be in the barn or in the cathedral, silently and quietly at the street door, or in the Sunday-school or in the classes. O Lord, bless Thy work. Hear also prayers that have been put up by wives for their husbands, children for their parents, parents for their children. Let the holy service of prayer never cease, and let the intercession be accepted of God, for Jesus Christ's sake. Amen.

*Spurgeon considered his* Treasury of David *to be the masterpiece of his literary works, and many are inclined to agree with him. He spent over twenty years writing its seven volumes that amounted to some two million words and were published volume-by-volume from 1870 to 1886. It contained "an original exposition of the book, a collection of illustrative extracts from the whole range of literature, a series of homiletical hints upon almost every verse and a list of writers upon each psalm." One condenser of the work has said that it was much more than a mere commentary on the Psalms: "Truly it may be termed a theological anthology of the whole realm of Christian truth."*

*His commentary on Psalm 119 was published separately and called "The Golden Alphabet." The selection presented here is the original exposition portion of his commentary on the first eight verses of Psalm 119.*

CHAPTER ELEVEN

## *Psalm One Hundred and Nineteen—Verses 1 to 8*

1 Blessed *are* the undefiled in the way, who walk in the law of the LORD.

2 Blessed *are* they that keep his testimonies, *and that* seek him with the whole heart.

3 They also do no iniquity: they walk in his ways.

4 Thou hast commanded *us* to keep thy precepts diligently.

5 O that my ways were directed to keep thy statutes!

6 Then shall I not be ashamed, when I have respect unto all thy commandments.

7 I will praise thee with uprightness of heart, when I shall have learned thy righteous judgments.

8 I will keep thy statutes: O forsake me not utterly.

These first eight verses are taken up with a contemplation of the blessedness which comes through keeping the statutes of the Lord. The subject is treated in a devout manner rather than in a didactic style. Heart-fellowship with God is enjoyed through a love of that word which is God's way of communing with the soul by his Holy Spirit. Prayer and praise and all sorts of devotional acts and feelings gleam through the verses like beams of sunlight through an olive grove. You are not only instructed, but influenced to holy emotion, and helped to express the same.

Lovers of God's holy words are blessed, because they are preserved from defilement (verse 1), because they are made practically holy (verses 2 and 3), and are led to follow after God sincerely and intensely (verse 2). It is seen that this holy walking must be desirable because God commands it (verse 4); therefore the pious soul prays for it (verse 5), and feels that its comfort and courage must depend upon obtaining it (verse 6). In the prospect of answered prayer, yea, while the prayer is being answered the heart is full of thankfulness (verse 7), and is fixed in solemn resolve not to miss the blessing if the Lord will give enabling grace (verse 8).

The changes are rung upon the words *"way"*— "undefiled in the way," "walk in his ways," "O that my ways were directed"; *"keep"*—"keep his testimonies," "keep thy precepts diligently," "directed to keep," "I will keep"; and *"walk"*—"walk in the law," "walk in his ways." Yet there is no tautology, nor is the same thought repeated, though to the careless reader it may seem so.

The change from statements about others and about the Lord to more personal dealing with God begins in the third verse, and becomes more clear as we advance, till in the later verses the communion becomes most intense and soul moving. O that every reader may feel the glow.

## "Blessed"

The psalmist is so enraptured with the word of God

that he regards it as his highest ideal of blessedness to be conformed to it. He has gazed on the beauties of the perfect law, and, as if this verse were the sum and outcome of all his emotions, he exclaims, "Blessed is the man whose life is the practical transcript of the will of God." True religion is not cold and dry; it has its exclamations and raptures. We not only judge the keeping of God's law to be a wise and proper thing, but we are warmly enamored of its holiness, and cry out in adoring wonder, "Blessed are the undefiled!" meaning thereby, that we eagerly desire to become such ourselves, and wish for no greater happiness than to be perfectly holy. It may be that the writer labored under a sense of his own faultiness, and therefore envied the blessedness of those whose walk had been more pure and clean; indeed, the very contemplation of the perfect law of the Lord upon which he now entered was quite enough to make him bemoan his own imperfections, and sigh for the blessedness of an undefiled walk.

True religion is always practical, for it does not permit us to delight ourselves in a perfect rule without exciting in us a longing to be conformed to it in our daily lives. A blessing belongs to those who hear and read and understand the word of the Lord; yet is it a far greater blessing to be actually obedient to it, and to carry out in our walk and conversation what we learn in our searching of the Scriptures. Purity in our way and walk is the truest blessedness.

This first verse is not only a preface to the whole psalm, but it may also be regarded as the text upon which the rest is a discourse. It is similar to the benediction of the first Psalm, which is set in the forefront of the entire book: there is a likeness between this 119th Psalm and the Psalter, and this is one point of it, that it begins with a benediction. In this, too, we see some foreshadowing of the Son of David, who began his great sermon as David began his great psalm. It is well to open our mouth with blessings. When we cannot bestow them, we can show the way of obtaining them, and even if we do not yet possess them ourselves, it may be profitable to comtemplate them, that our desires may be excited, and our souls moved to seek after them. Lord, if I am not yet so blessed to be among the undefiled in thy way, yet I will think much of the happiness which these enjoy, and set it before me as my life's ambition.

As David thus begins his psalm, so should young men begin their lives, so should new converts commence their profession, so should all Christians begin every day. Settle it in your hearts as a first postulate and sure rule of practical science that holiness is happiness, and that it is our wisdom first to seek the Kingdom of God and his righteousness. Well begun is half done. To start with a true idea of blessedness is beyond measure important. Man began with being blessed in his innocence, and if our fallen race is ever to be blessed again, it must find it where it lost it at the beginning, namely, in conformity to the command of the Lord.

*"The undefiled in the way."* They are in the way, the right way, the way of the Lord, and they keep that way, walking with holy carefulness and washing their feet daily, lest they be found spotted by the flesh. They enjoy great blessedness in their own souls; indeed, they have a foretaste of heaven where the blessedness lieth much in being absolutely undefiled; and could they continue utterly and altogether without defilement, doubtless they would have the days of heaven upon the earth. Outward evil would little hurt us if we were entirely rid of the evil

of sin, an attainment which with the best of us lies still in the region of desire, and is not yet fully reached, though we have so clear a view of it that we see it to be blessedness itself; and therefore we eagerly press towards it.

He whose life is in a gospel sense undefiled, is blessed, because he could never have reached this point if a thousand blessings had not already been bestowed on him. By nature we are defiled and out of the way, and we must therefore have been washed in the atoning blood to remove defilement, and we must have been converted by the power of the Holy Ghost, or we should not have been turned into the way of peace, nor be undefiled in it. Nor is this all, for the continual power of grace is needed to keep a believer in the right way, and to preserve him from pollution. All the blessings of the covenant must have been in a measure poured upon those who from day to day have been enabled to perfect holiness in the fear of the Lord. Their way is the evidence of their being the blessed of the Lord.

David speaks of a high degree of blessedness; for some are in the way, and are true servants of God, but they are as yet faulty in many ways and bring defilement upon themselves. Others who walk in the light more fully, and maintain closer communion with God, are enabled to keep themselves unspotted from the world, and these enjoy far more peace and joy than their less watchful brethren. Doubtless, the more complete our sanctification the more intense our blessedness. Christ is our way, and we are not only alive in Christ, but we are to live in Christ; the sorrow is that we bespatter his holy way with our selfishness, self-exaltation, wilfulness, and carnality, and so we miss a great measure of the blessedness which is in him as our way. A believer who errs is still

saved, but the joy of his salvation is not experienced by
him; he is rescued but not enriched, greatly borne with,
but not greatly blessed.

How easily may defilement come upon us even in our
holy things, yea, even *in the way.* We may even come from
public or private worship with defilement upon the conscience gathered when we were on our knees. There was
no floor to the tabernacle but the desert sand, and hence
the priests at the altar were under frequent necessity to
wash their feet, and by the kind foresight of their God,
the laver stood ready for their cleansing, even as for us
our Lord Jesus still stands ready to wash our feet, that
we may be clean every whit. Thus our text sets forth the
blessedness of the apostles in the upper room when
Jesus had said of them, "Ye are clean."

What blessedness awaits those who follow the Lamb
whithersoever he goeth, and are preserved from the evil
which is in the world through lust. These shall be the
envy of all mankind "in that day." Though now they despise them as precise fanatics and Puritans, the most
prosperous of sinners shall then wish that they could
change places with them. O my soul, seek thou thy blessedness in following hard after thy Lord, who was holy,
harmless, undefiled; for there hast thou found peace
hitherto, and there wilt thou find it for ever.

*"Who walk in the law of the Lord."* In them is found
habitual holiness. Their walk, their common everyday
life is obedience unto the Lord. They live by rule, that
rule the command of the Lord God. Whether they eat or
drink, or whatsoever they do, they do all in the name of
their great Master and Exemplar. To them religion is
nothing out of the way, it is their everyday walk: it
molds their common actions as well as their special devotions. This ensures blessedness. He who walks in

God's law walks in God's company, and he must be blessed; he has God's smile, God's strength, God's secret with him, and how can he be otherwise than blessed?

The holy life is a walk, a steady progress, a quiet advance, a lasting continuance. Enoch walked with God. Good men always long to be better, and hence they go forward. Good men are never idle, and hence they do not lie down or loiter, but they are still walking onward to their desired end. They are not hurried, and worried, and flurried, and so they keep the even tenor of their way, walking steadily towards heaven; and they are not in perplexity as to how to conduct themselves, for they have a perfect rule, which they are happy to walk by. The law of the Lord is not irksome to them; its commandments are not grievous, and its restrictions are not slavish in their esteem. It does not appear to them to be an impossible law, theoretically admirable but practically absurd, but they walk by it and in it. They do not consult it now and then as a sort of rectifier of their wanderings, but they use it as a chart for their daily sailing, a map of the road for their life-journey.

Nor do they ever regret that they have entered upon the path of obedience, else they would leave it, and that without difficulty, for a thousand temptations offer them opportunity to return; their continued walk in the law of the Lord is their best testimony to the blessedness of such a condition of life. Yes, they are blessed even now. The psalmist himself bore witness to the fact: he had tried and proved it, and wrote it down, as a fact which defied all denial. Here it stands in the forefront of David's *magnum opus,* written on the topmost line of his greatest psalm—"BLESSED ARE THEY WHO WALK IN THE LAW OF THE LORD." Rough may be the way, stern the rule, hard the discipline,—all these we know and more,—but a thousand heaped-up blessednesses are still found in godly living, for which we bless the Lord.

We have in this verse blessed persons who enjoy five blessed things, a blessed way, blessed purity, a blessed law, given by a blessed Lord, and a blessed walk therein; to which we may add the blessed testimony of the Holy Ghost given in this very passage that they are in very deed the blessed of the Lord.

The blessedness which is thus set before us we must aim at, but we must not think to obtain it without earnest effort. David has a great deal to say about it; his discourse in this psalm is long and solemn, and it is a hint to us that the way of perfect obedience is not learned in a day; there must be precept upon precept, line upon line, and after efforts long enough to be compared with the 176 verses of this psalm we may still have to cry, "I have gone astray like a lost sheep; seek they servant; for I do not forget thy commandments."

It must, however, be our plan to keep the word of the Lord much upon our minds; for this discourse upon blessedness has for its pole-star the testimony of the Lord, and only by daily communion with the Lord by his word can we hope to learn his way, to be purged from defilement, and to be made to walk in his statutes. We set out upon this exposition with blessedness before us; we see the way to it, and we know where the law of it is to be found: let us pray that as we pursue our meditation we may grow into the habit and walk of obedience, and so feel the blessedness of which we read.

## "Blessed Are They That Keep His Testimonies"

What! A second blessing? Yes, they are doubly blessed whose outward life is supported by an inward zeal for

God's glory. In the first verse we had an undefiled way, and it was taken for granted that the purity in the way was not mere surface work, but was attended by the inward truth and life which comes of divine grace. Here that which was implied is expressed. Blessedness is ascribed to those who treasure up the testimonies of the Lord: in which is implied that they search the Scriptures, that they come to an understanding of them, that they love them, and then that they continue in the practice of them. We must first get a thing before we can keep it. In order to keep it well we must get a firm grip of it: we cannot keep in the heart that which we have not heartily embraced by the affections. God's word is his witness or testimony to grand and important truths which concern himself and our relation to him: this we should desire to know; knowing it, we should believe it; believing it, we should love it; and loving it, we should hold it fast against all comers.

There is a doctrinal keeping of the word when we are ready to die for its defense, and a practical keeping of it when we actually live under its power. Revealed truth is precious as diamonds, and should be kept or treasured up in the memory and in the heart as jewels in a casket, or as the law was kept in the ark; this however is not enough, for it is meant for practical use, and therefore it must be kept or followed, as men keep to a path, or to a line of business. If we keep God's testimonies they will keep us; they will keep us right in opinion, comfortable in spirit, holy in conversation, and hopeful in expectation. If they were ever worth having—and no thoughtful person will question that—then they are worth keeping; their designed effect does not come through a temporary seizure of them, but by a persevering keeping of them: "in keeping of them there is great reward."

We are bound to keep with all care the word of God, because it is *his* testimonies. He gave them to us, but they are still his own. We are to keep them as a watchman guards his master's house, as a steward husbands his lord's goods, as a shepherd keeps his employer's flock. We shall have to give an account, for we are put in trust with the gospel, and woe to us if we be found unfaithful. We cannot fight a good fight, nor finish our course, unless we keep the faith. To this end the Lord must keep us: only those who are kept by the power of God unto salvation will ever be able to keep his testimonies.

What a blessedness is therefore evidenced and testified by a careful belief in God's word, and a continual obedience thereunto. God has blessed them, is blessing them, and will bless them for ever. That blessedness which David saw in others he realized for himself, for in verse 168 he says, "I have kept thy precepts and thy testimonies," and in verses 54 to 56 he traces his joyful songs and happy memories to this same keeping of the law, and he confesses, "This I had because I kept thy precepts." Doctrines which we teach to others we should experience for ourselves.

*"And that seek him with the whole heart."* Those who keep the Lord's testimonies are sure to seek after himself. If his word is precious we may be sure that he himself is still more so. Personal dealing with a personal God is the longing of all those who have allowed the word of the Lord to have its full effect upon them. If we once really know the power of the gospel we must seek the God of the gospel. "O that I knew where I might find HIM," will be our whole-hearted cry. See the growth which these sentences indicate: first, in the way, then walking in it, then finding and keeping the treasure of

truth, and to crown all, seeking after the Lord of the way himself. Note also that the further a soul advances in grace the more spiritual and divine are its longings; an outward walk does not content the gracious soul, nor even the treasured testimonies; it reaches out in due time after God himself, and when it in a measure finds him, still yearns for more of him, and seeks him still.

Seeking after God signifies a desire to commune with him more closely, to follow him more fully, to enter into more perfect union with his mind and will, to promote his glory, and to realize completely all that he is to holy hearts. The blessed man has God already, and for this reason he seeks him. This may seem a contradiction: it is only a paradox.

God is not truly sought by the cold researches of the brain: we must seek him with the heart. Love reveals itself to love: God manifests his heart to the heart of his people. It is in vain that we endeavor to comprehend him by reason; we must apprehend him by affection. But the heart must not be divided with many objects if the Lord is to be sought by us. God is one, and we shall not know him till our heart is one. A broken heart need not be distressed at this, for no heart is so whole in its seekings after God as a heart which is broken, whereof every fragment sighs and cries after the great Father's face. It is the divided heart which the doctrine of the text censures, and strange to say, in scriptural phraseology, a heart may be divided and not broken, and it may be broken but not divided; and yet again it may be broken and be whole, and it never can be whole until it is broken. When our whole heart seeks the holy God in Christ Jesus, it has come to him of whom it is written, "as many as touched him were made perfectly whole."

That which the psalmist admires in this verse he

claims in the tenth, where he says, "With my whole heart have I sought thee." It is well when admiration of a virtue leads to the attainment of it. Those who do not believe in the blessedness of seeking the Lord will not be likely to arouse their hearts to the pursuit, but he who calls another blessed because of the grace which he sees in him is on the way to gaining the same grace for himself.

If those who *seek* the Lord are blessed, what shall be said of those who actually dwell with him and know that he is theirs?

> To those who fall, how kind thou art!
>   How good to those who seek
> But what to those who find? Ah! this
>   Nor tongue nor pen can show!
> The love of Jesus—what it is,
>   None but his loved ones know.

## "They Also Do No Iniquity"

Blessed indeed would those men be of whom this could be asserted without reserve and without explanation: we shall have reached the region of pure blessedness when we altogether cease from sin. Those who follow the word of God do no iniquity, the rule is perfect, and if it be constantly followed no fault will arise. Life, to the outward observer, at any rate, lies much in doing, and he who in his doings never swerves from equity, both towards God and man, has hit upon the way of perfection, and we may be sure that his heart is right. See how a whole heart leads to the avoidance of evil, for the psalmist says, "That seek him with the whole heart. They also do no iniquity."

We fear that no man can claim to be absolutely without sin, and yet we trust there are many who do not designedly, wilfully, knowingly, and continuously do anything that is wicked, ungodly, or unjust. Grace keeps the life righteous as to act even when the Christian has to bemoan the transgressions of the heart. Judged as men should be judged by their fellows, according to such just rules as men make for men, the true people of God do no iniquity: they are honest, upright, and chaste, and touching justice and morality they are blameless. Therefore are they happy.

*"They walk in his ways."* They attend not only to the great main highway of the law, but to the smaller paths of the particular precepts. As they will perpetrate no sin of commission, so do they labor to be free from every sin of omission. It is not enough to them to be blameless, they wish also to be actively righteous. A hermit may escape into solitude that he may do no iniquity, but a saint lives in society that he may serve his God by walking in his ways.

We must be positively as well as negatively right: we shall not long keep the second unless we attend to the first, for men will be walking one way or another, and if they do not follow the path of God's law they will soon do iniquity. The surest way to abstain from evil is to be fully occupied in doing good. This verse describes believers as they exist among us: although they have their faults and infirmities, yet they hate evil, and will not permit themselves to do it; they love the ways of truth, right and true godliness, and habitually they walk therein. They do not claim to be absolutely perfect except in their desires, and there they are pure indeed, for they pant to be kept from all sin, and to be led into all holiness.

## "Thou Hast Commanded Us to Keep Thy Precepts Diligently"

So that when we have done all we are unprofitable servants, we have done only that which it was our duty to have done, seeing we have our Lord's command for it. God's precepts require *careful* obedience: there is no keeping them by accident. Some give to God a careless service, a sort of hit or miss obedience, but the Lord has not commanded such service, nor will he accept it. His law demands the love of all our heart, soul, mind, and strength; and a careless religion has none of these.

We are also called to *zealous* obedience. We are to keep the precepts abundantly: the vessels of obedience should be filled to the brim, and the command carried out to the full of its meaning. As a man diligent in business arouses himself to do as much trade as he can, so must we be eager to serve the Lord as much as possible. Nor must we spare pains to do so, for a diligent obedience will also be *laborious and self-denying*. Those who are diligent in business rise up early and sit up late, and deny themselves much of comfort and repose. They are not soon tired, or if they are they persevere even with aching brow and weary eyes. So should we serve the Lord. Such a Master deserves diligent servants; such service he demands, and will be content with nothing less. How seldom do men render it, and hence many through their negligence miss the double blessing spoken of in this psalm.

Some are diligent in superstition and will worship; be it ours to be diligent in keeping God's precepts. It is no use travelling fast if we are not in the right road. Men have been diligent in a losing business, and the more they have traded the more they have lost: this is bad enough in commerce, we cannot afford to have it so in our religion.

God has not commanded us to be diligent in *making* precepts, but in *keeping* them. Some bind yokes upon their own necks, and make bonds and rules for others: but the wise course is to be satisfied with the rules of holy Scripture, and to strive to keep them all, in all places, towards all men, and in all respects. If we do not this, we may become eminent in our own religion, but we shall not have kept the command of God, nor shall we be accepted of him.

The psalmist began with the third person: he is now coming near home, and has already reached the first person plural, according to our version; we shall soon hear him crying out personally for himself. As the heart glows with love to holiness, we long to have a personal interest in it. The word of God is a heart-affecting book, and when we begin to sing its praises it soon comes home to us, and sets us praying to be ourselves conformed to its teachings.

### "O That My Ways Were Directed to Keep Thy Statutes!"

Divine commands should direct us in the subject of our prayers. We cannot of ourselves keep God's statutes as he would have them kept, and yet we long to do so: what resort have we but prayer? We must ask the Lord to work our works in us, or we shall never work out his commandments. This verse is a sigh of regret because the psalmist feels that he has not kept the precepts diligently, it is a cry of weakness appealing for help to one who can aid, it is a request of bewilderment from one who has lost his way and would fain be directed in it, and it is a petition of faith from one who loves God and trusts in him for grace.

Our ways are by nature opposed to the way of God, and must be turned by the Lord's direction in another direction from that which they originally take or they will lead us down to destruction. God can direct the mind and will without violating our free agency, and he will do so in answer to prayer; in fact, he has begun the work already in those who are heartily praying after the fashion of this verse. It is for present holiness that the desire arises in the heart. O that it were so now with me: but future persevering holiness is also meant, for he longs for grace to keep henceforth and for ever the statutes of the Lord.

The sigh of the text is really a prayer, though it does not exactly take that form. Desires and longings are of the essence of supplication, and it little matters what shape they take. "O that" is as acceptable a prayer as "Our Father."

One would hardly have expected a prayer for direction; rather should we have looked for a petition for enabling. Can we not direct ourselves? What if we cannot row, we can steer. The psalmist herein confesses that even for the smallest part of his duty he felt unable without grace. He longed for the Lord to influence his will, as well as to strengthen his hands. We want a rod to point out the way as much as a staff to support us in it.

The longing of the text is prompted by admiration of the blessedness of holiness, by a contemplation of the righteous man's beauty of character, and by a reverent awe of the command of God. It is a personal application to the writer's own case of the truths which he had been considering. "O that *my* ways," etc. It were well if all who hear and read the word would copy this example and turn all that they hear into prayer. We should have more keepers of the statutes if we had more who sighed and cried after the grace to do so.

## "Then Shall I Not Be Ashamed"

He had known shame, and here he rejoices in the prospect of being freed from it. Sin brings shame, and when sin is gone, the reason for being ashamed is banished. What a deliverance this is, for to some men death is preferable to shame! *"When I have respect unto all thy commandments."* When he respects God he shall respect himself and be respected. Whenever we err we prepare ourselves for confusion of face and sinking of heart: if no one else is ashamed of me I shall be ashamed of myself if I do iniquity. Our first parents never knew shame till they made the acquaintance of the old serpent, and it never left them till their gracious God had covered them with sacrificial skins. Disobedience made them naked and ashamed. We, ourselves, will always have cause for shame till every sin is vanquished, and every duty is observed. When we pay a continual and universal respect to the will of the Lord, then we shall be able to look ourselves in the face in the looking-glass of the law, and we shall not blush at the sight of men or devils, however eager their malice may be to lay somewhat to our charge.

Many suffer from excessive diffidence, and this verse suggests a cure. An abiding sense of duty will make us bold, we shall be afraid to be afraid. No shame in the presence of man will hinder us when the fear of God has taken full possession of our minds. When we are on the king's highway by daylight, and are engaged upon royal business, we need ask no man's leave. It would be a dishonor to a king to be ashamed of his livery and his service; no such shame should ever crimson the cheek of a Christian, nor will it if he has due reverence for the Lord his God. There is nothing to be ashamed of in a holy life; a man may be ashamed of his pride, ashamed of his wealth, ashamed of his own children, but he will never be ashamed of having in all things regarded the will of the Lord his God.

It is worthy of remark that David promises himself no immunity from shame till he has carefully paid homage to all the precepts. Mind that word *"all,"* and leave not one command out of your respect. Partial obedience still leaves us liable to be called to account for those commands which we have neglected. A man may have a thousand virtues, and yet a single failing may cover him with shame.

To a poor sinner who is buried in despair, it may seem a very unlikely thing that he should ever be delivered from shame. He blushes, and is confounded, and feels that he can never lift up his face again. Let him read these words: "Then shall I not be ashamed." David is not dreaming, nor picturing an impossible case. Be assured, dear friend, that the Holy Spirit can renew in you the image of God, so that you shall yet look up without fear. O for sanctification to direct us in God's way, for then shall we have boldness both towards God and his people, and shall no more crimson with confusion.

## "I Will Praise Thee"

From prayer to praise is never a long or a difficult journey. Be sure that he who prays for holiness will one day praise for happiness. Shame having vanished, silence is broken, and the formerly silent man declares, "I will praise thee." He cannot but promise praise while he seeks sanctification. Mark how well he knows upon what head to set the crown. "I will praise *thee*." He would himself be praiseworthy, but he counts God alone worthy of praise. By the sorrow and shame of sin he measures his obligations to the Lord who would teach him the art of living as that he should clean escape from his former misery.

*"With uprightness of heart."* His heart would be upright if the Lord would teach him, and then it should praise its teacher. There is such a thing as false and feigned praise, and this the Lord abhors; but there is no music like that which comes from a pure soul which standeth in its integrity. Heart praise is required, uprightness in that heart, and teaching to make the heart upright. An upright heart is sure to bless the Lord, for grateful adoration is a part of its uprightness; no man can be right unless he is upright towards God, and this involves the rendering to him the praise which is his due.

*"When I shall have learned thy righteous judgments."* We must learn to praise, learn that we may praise, and praise when we have learned. If we are ever to learn, the Lord must teach us, and especially upon such a subject as his judgments, for they are a great deep. While these are passing before our eyes, and we are learning from them, we ought to praise God, for the original is not, "when I have learned," but, "in my learning." While yet I am a scholar I will be a chorister: my upright heart shall praise thine uprightness, my purified judgment shall admire thy judgments. God's providence is a book full of teaching, and to those whose hearts are right it is a music book, out of which they chant to Jehovah's praise. God's word is full of the record of his righteous providences, and as we read it we feel compelled to burst forth into expressions of holy delight and ardent praise.

When we both read of God's judgments and become joyful partakers in them, we are doubly moved to song—song in which there is neither formality, nor hypocrisy, nor lukewarmness, for the heart is upright in the presentation of its praise.

## "I Will Keep Thy Statutes"

A calm resolve. When praise calms down into solid resolution it is well with the soul. Zeal which spends itself in singing, and leaves no practical residuum of holy living, is little worth: "I will praise" should be coupled with "I will keep." This firm resolve is by no means boastful, like Peter's humble prayer for divine help, *O forsake me not utterly.* Feeling his own incapacity he trembles lest he should be left to himself, and this fear is increased by the horror which he has of falling into sin. The "I will keep" sounds rightly enough now that the humble cry is heard with it. This is a happy amalgam: resolution and dependence.

We meet with those who to all appearance humbly pray, but there is no force of character, no decision in them, and consequently the pleading of the closet is not embodied in the life: on the other hand, we meet with abundance of resolve attended with an entire absence of dependence upon God, and this makes as poor a character as the former. The Lord grant us to have such a blending of excellences that we may be "perfect and entire, wanting nothing."

This prayer is one which is certain to be heard, for assuredly it must be highly pleasing to God to see a man set upon obeying his will, and therefore it must be most agreeable to him to be present with such a person, and to help him in his endeavors. How can he forsake one who does not forsake his law?

The peculiar dread which tinges this prayer with a somber hue is the fear of utter forsaking. Well may the soul cry out against such a calamity. To be left, that we may discover our weakness, is a sufficient trial: to be altogether forsaken would be ruin and death. Hiding the face in a little wrath for a moment brings us very low: an absolute desertion would land us ultimately in the lowest hell. But the Lord never has utterly forsaken his servants, and he never will, blessed be his name. If we long to keep his statutes he will keep us; yea, his grace will keep us keeping his law.

There is rather a descent from the mount of benediction with which the first verse began to the almost wail of this eighth verse, yet this is spiritually a growth, for from admiration of goodness we have come to a burning longing after God and communion with him, and an intense horror lest it should not be enjoyed. The sigh of verse 5 is now supplanted by an actual prayer from the depths of a heart conscious of its undesert, and its entire dependence upon divine love. The two "I wills" needed to be seasoned with some such lowly petition, or it might have been thought that the good man's dependence was in some degree fixed upon his own determination. He presents his resolutions like a sacrifice, but he cries to heaven for the fire.

*Spurgeon's theology was distinctly Calvinistic, and he labored much to defend his views. In contrast to the hyper-Calvinists, whom he often argued against, Spurgeon's Calvinistic theology led him to a vigorously evangelistic approach. "A Defense of Calvinism" is the thirteenth chapter of the second volume of his autobiography, which was compiled by his widow and published in 1897.*

*Elsewhere Spurgeon wrote: "We use the term 'Calvinism' for shortness. The doctrine which is called 'Calvinism' did not spring from Calvin; we believe that it sprang from the great founder of all truth." In "A Defense of Calvinism," Spurgeon eloquently presents and defends Calvinism, and, as always in Spurgeon's works, grace is one of his primary themes.*

## CHAPTER TWELVE

---

# *A Defense of Calvinism*

It is a great thing to begin the Christian life by believing good solid doctrine. Some people have received twenty different "gospels" in as many years; how many more they will accept before they get to their journey's end, it would be difficult to predict. I thank God that He early taught me *the* gospel, and I have been so perfectly satisfied with it, that I do not want to know any other. Constant change of creed is sure loss. If a tree has to be taken up two or three times a year, you will not need to build a very large loft in which to store the apples. When people are always shifting their doctrinal principles, they are not likely to bring forth much fruit to the glory of God.

It is good for young believers to begin with a firm hold upon those great fundamental doctrines which the Lord has taught in His Word. Why, if I believed what some preach about the temporary, trumpery salvation which only lasts for a time, I would scarcely be at all grateful for it; but when I know that those whom God saves He saves with an everlasting salvation, when I know that He gives to them an everlasting righteousness, when I know that He settles them on an everlasting foundation of everlasting love, and that He will bring them to His everlasting kingdom, oh, then I do wonder, and I am astonished that such a blessing as this should ever have been given to me!

> Pause, my soul! adore, and wonder!
> Ask, "Oh, why such love to me?"
> Grace hath put me in the number
> Of the Savior's family:
> Hallelujah!
> Thanks, eternal thanks, to Thee!

## A Personal Testimony

I suppose there are persons whose minds naturally incline towards the doctrine of free-will. I can only say that mine inclines as naturally towards the doctrines of sovereign grace. Sometimes, when I see some of the worst characters in the street, I feel as if my heart must burst forth in tears of gratitude that God has never let me act as they have done! I have thought, if God had left me alone, and had not touched me by His grace, what a great sinner I should have been! I should have run to the utmost lengths of sin, dived into the very depths of evil, nor should I have stopped at any vice or folly, if God had not restrained me. I feel that I should have been a very king of sinners, if God had let me alone. I cannot understand the reason why I am saved, except upon the ground that God would have it so. I cannot, if I look ever so earnestly, discover any kind of reason in myself why I should be a partaker of divine grace. If I am not at this moment without Christ, it is only because Christ Jesus would have His will with me, and that will was that I should be with Him where He is, and should share His glory. I can put the crown nowhere but upon the head of Him whose mighty grace has saved me from going down into the pit.

Looking back on my past life, I can see that the dawning of it all was of God; of God effectively. I took no torch with which to light the sun, but the sun enlightened me. I did not commence my spiritual life—no, I rather kicked, and struggled against the things of the Spirit: when He drew me, for a time I did not run after Him: there was a natural hatred in my soul of everything holy and good. Wooings were lost upon me—warnings were cast to the wind—thunders were despised; and as for the whispers of His love, they were rejected as being less than nothing and vanity. But, sure I am, I can say now, speaking on behalf of myself, "He only is my salvation." It was He who turned my heart, and brought me down on my knees before Him. I can in very deed, say with Doddridge and Toplady—

> Grace taught my soul to pray,
> And made my eyes o'erflow;

and coming to this moment, I can add—

> 'Tis grace *has* kept me to this day,
> And will not let me go.

Well can I remember the manner in which I learned the doctrines of grace in a single instant. Born, as all of us are by nature, an Arminian, I still believed the old

257

things I had heard continually from the pulpit, and did not see the grace of God. When I was coming to Christ, I thought I was doing it all myself, and though I sought the Lord earnestly, I had no idea the Lord was seeking me. I do not think the young convert is at first aware of this. I can recall the very day and hour when first I received those truths in my own soul—when they were, as John Bunyan says, burnt into my heart as with a hot iron, and I can recollect how I felt that I had grown on a sudden from a babe into a man—that I had made progress in Scriptural knowledge, through having found, once for all, the clue to the truth of God.

One week-night, when I was sitting in the house of God, I was not thinking much about the preacher's sermon, for I did not believe it. The thought struck me, *"How did you come to be a Christian?"* I sought the Lord. *"But how did you come to seek the Lord?"* The truth flashed across my mind in a moment—I should not have sought Him unless there had been some previous influence in my mind to *make me* seek Him. I prayed, thought I, but then I asked myself, *How came I to pray?* I was induced to pray by reading the Scriptures. *How came I to read the Scriptures?* I did read them, but what led me to do so? Then, in a moment, I saw that God was at the bottom of it all, and that He was the Author of my faith, and so the whole doctrine of grace opened up to me, and from that doctrine I have not departed to this day, and I desire to make this my constant confession. "I ascribe my change wholly to God."

I once attended a service where the text happened to be, "*He* shall choose our inheritance for us;" and the good man who occupied the pulpit was more than a little of an Arminian. Therefore, when he commenced, he said, "This passage refers entirely to our temporal inheritance, it has nothing whatever to do with our everlasting destiny, for," said he, "we do not want Christ to choose for us in the matter of heaven or hell. It is so plain and easy, that every man who has a grain of common sense will choose heaven, and any person would know better than to choose hell. We have no need of any superior intelligence, or any greater Being, to choose heaven or hell for us. It is left to our own free-will, and we have enough wisdom given us, sufficiently correct means to judge for ourselves," and therefore, as he very logically inferred, there was no necessity for Jesus Christ, or anyone, to make a choice for us. We could choose the inheritance for ourselves without any assistance. "Ah!" I thought, "but, my good brother, it may be very true that we *could,* but I think we should want something more than common sense before we *should* choose aright."

## God's Election

First, let me ask, must we not all of us admit an over-ruling providence, and the appointment of Jehovah's hand, as to the means whereby we came into this world? Those men who think that, afterwards, we are left to our own free-will to choose this one or the other to direct our steps, must admit that our entrance into the world was not of our own will, but that God had then to choose for us. What circumstances were those in our power which led us to elect certain persons to be our parents? Had we anything to do with it? Did not God Himself appoint our parents, native place, and friends? Could He not have caused me to be born with the skin of the Hottentot, brought forth by a filthy mother who would nurse me in her "kraal", and teach me to bow down to pagan gods, quite as easily as to have given me a pious mother, who would each morning and night bend her knee in prayer on my behalf? Or, might He not, if He had pleased, have given me some profligate to have been my parent, from whose lips I might have early heard fearful, filthy, and obscene language? Might He not have placed me where I should have had a drunken father, who would have immured me in a very dungeon of ignorance, and brought me up in the chains of crime? Was it not God's providence that I had so happy a lot, that both my parents were His children, and endeavored to train me up in the fear of the Lord?

John Newton used to tell a whimsical story, and laugh at it, too, of a good woman who said, in order to prove the doctrine of election, "Ah! sir, the Lord must have loved me before I was born, or else He would not have seen anything in me to love afterwards." I am sure it is true in my case; I believe the doctrine of election, because I am quite certain that, if God had not chosen me, I should never have chosen Him; and I am sure He chose me before I was born, or else He never would have chosen me afterwards; and He must have elected me for reasons unknown to me, for I never could find any reason in myself why He should have looked upon me with special love. So I am forced to accept that great Biblical doctrine.

I recollect an Arminian brother telling me that he had read the Scriptures through a score or more times, and could never find the doctrine of election in them. He added that he was sure he would have done so if it had been there, for he read the Word on his knees. I said to him, "I think you read the Bible in a very uncomfortable posture, and if you had read it in your easy chair, you would have been more likely to understand it. Pray, by all means, and the more, the better, but it is a piece of superstition to think there is anything in the posture in which a man puts himself for reading: and as to reading through the Bible twenty times without having found anything about the doctrine of election, the wonder is that you found anything at all: you must have galloped through it at such a rate that you were not likely to have any intelligible idea of the meaning of the Scriptures."

If it would be marvellous to see one river leap up from the earth full-grown, what would it be to gaze upon a vast spring from which all the rivers of the earth should at once come bubbling up, a million of them born at a birth? What a vision would it be! Who can conceive it. And yet the love of God is that fountain, from which all the rivers of mercy, which have ever gladdened our race—all the rivers of grace in time, and of glory here-after—take their rise. My soul, stand thou at that sacred fountain-head, and adore and magnify for ever and ever God, even our Father, who hath loved us!

In the very beginning, when this great universe lay in the mind of God, like unborn forests in the acorn cup; long ere the echoes awoke the solitudes; before the mountains were brought forth; and long ere the light flashed through the sky, God loved His chosen creatures. Before there was any created being—when the ether was not fanned by an angel's wing, when space itself had not an existence, when there was nothing save God alone— even then, in that loneliness of deity, and in that deep quiet and profundity, His bowels moved with love for His chosen. Their names were written on His heart, and then were they dear to His soul. Jesus loved His people before the foundation of the world—even from eternity! and when He called me by His grace, He said to me, "I have loved *thee* with an everlasting love: therefore with loving-kindness have I drawn thee."

Then, in the fulness of time, He purchased me with

His blood; He let His heart run out in one deep gaping wound for me long ere I loved Him. Yea, when He first came to me, did I not spurn Him? When He knocked at the door, and asked for entrance, did I not drive Him away, and do despite to His grace? Ah! I can remember that I full often did so until, at last, by the power of His effectual grace, He said, "I must, I will come in;" and then He turned my heart, and made me love Him. But even till now I should have resisted Him, had it not been for His grace.

Well, then, since He purchased me when I was dead in sins, does it not follow, as a consequence necessary and logical, that He must have loved me first? Did my Savior die for me because I believed on Him? No; I was not then in existence; I had then no being. Could the Savior, therefore, have died because I had faith, when I myself was not yet born? Could that have been possible? Could that have been the origin of the Savior's love towards me? Oh! no; my Savior died for me long before I believed.

"But," says someone, "He foresaw that you would have faith; and, therefore, He loved you." What did He foresee about my faith? Did He foresee that I should get that faith myself, and that I should believe on Him of myself? No; Christ could not foresee that, because no Christian man will ever say that faith came of itself without the gift and without the working of the Holy Spirit. I have met with a great many believers, and talked with them about this matter; but I never knew one who could put his hand on his heart, and say, "I believed in Jesus without the assistance of the Holy Spirit."

I am bound to the doctrine of the depravity of the human heart, because I find myself depraved in heart, and have daily proofs that in my flesh there dwelleth no good thing. If God enters into covenant with unfallen man, man is so insignificant a creature that it must be an act of gracious condescension on the Lord's part; but if God enters into covenant with *sinful* man, he is then so offensive a creature that it must be, on God's part, an act of pure, free, rich, sovereign grace. When the Lord entered into covenant with me, I am sure that it was all of grace, nothing else but grace. When I remember what a den of unclean beasts and birds my heart was, and how strong was my unrenewed will, how obstinate and rebellious against the sovereignty of the divine rule, I always feel inclined to take the very lowest room in my Father's house, and when I enter heaven, it will be to go among the less than the least of all saints, and with the chief of sinners.

## Salvation Is of the Lord

The late lamented Mr. Denham has put, at the foot of his portrait, a most admirable text, "Salvation is of the Lord." That is just an epitome of Calvinism; it is the sum and substance of it. If anyone should ask me what I mean by a Calvinist, I should reply, "He is one who says, *Salvation is of the Lord.*" I cannot find in Scripture any other doctrine than this. It is the essence of the Bible. "He *only* is my rock and my salvation." Tell me anything contrary to this truth, and it will be a heresy; tell me a heresy, and I shall find its essence here, that it has departed from this great, this fundamental, this rock-truth, "God is my rock and my salvation." What is the heresy of Rome, but the addition of something to the perfect merits of Jesus Christ—the bringing in of the works of the flesh, to assist in our justification? And what is the heresy of Arminianism but the addition of something to the work of the Redeemer? Every heresy, if brought to the touchstone, will discover itself here.

I have my own private opinion that there is no such thing as preaching Christ and Him crucified, unless we preach what nowadays is called Calvinism. It is a nickname to call it Calvinism; Calvinism is the gospel, and nothing else. I do not believe we can preach the gospel, if we do not preach justification by faith, without works; nor unless we preach the sovereignty of God in His dispensation of grace; nor unless we exalt the electing, unchangeable, eternal, immutable, conquering love of Jehovah; nor do I think we can preach the gospel, unless we base it upon the special and particular redemption of His elect and chosen people which Christ wrought out upon the cross; nor can I comprehend a gospel which lets saints fall away after they are called, and suffers the children of God to be burned in the fires of damnation after having once believed in Jesus. Such a gospel I abhor.

> If ever it should come to pass,
>   That sheep of Christ might fall away,
> My fickle, feeble soul, alas!
>   Would fall a thousand times a day.

If one dear saint of God had perished, so might all; if one of the covenant ones be lost, so may all be; and then there is no gospel promise true, but the Bible is a lie, and there is nothing in it worth my acceptance, I will be an infidel at once when I can believe that a saint of God can ever fall finally. If God hath loved me once, then He will love me for ever. God has a master-mind; He arranged everything in His gigantic intellect long before He did it; and once having settled it, He never alters it, "This shall be done," saith He, and the iron hand of destiny marks it down, and it is brought to pass. "This is My purpose," and it stands, nor can earth or hell alter it. "This is My decree," saith He, "promulgate it, ye holy angels; rend it down from the gate of heaven, ye devils, if ye can; but ye cannot alter the decree, it shall stand for ever."

God altereth not His plans; why should He? He is Almighty, and therefore can perform His pleasure. Why should He? He is the All-wise, and therefore cannot have planned wrongly. Why should He? He is the everlasting God, and therefore cannot die before His plan is accomplished. Why should He change? Ye worthless atoms of earth, ephemera of a day, ye creeping insects upon this bay-leaf of existence, ye may change *your* plans, but He shall never, never change *His*. Has He told me that His plan is to save me? If so, I am for ever safe.

> My name from the palms of His hands
>     Eternity will not erase;
> Impress'd on His heart it remains,
>     In marks of indelible grace.

I do not know how some people, who believe that a Christian can fall from grace, manage to be happy. It must be a very commendable thing in them to be able to get through a day without despair. If I did not believe the doctrine of the final perseverance of the saints, I think I should be of all men the most miserable, because I should lack any ground of comfort. I could not say, whatever state of heart I came into, that I should be like a well-spring of water, whose stream fails not; I should rather have to take the comparison of an intermittent spring, that might stop on a sudden, or a reservoir, which I had no reason to expect would always be full.

I believe that the happiest of Christians and the truest of Christians are those who never dare to doubt God, but who take His Word simply as it stands, and believe it, and ask no questions, just feeling assured that if God has said it, it will be so. I bear my willing testimony that I have no reason, nor even the shadow of a reason, to doubt my Lord, and I challenge heaven, and earth, and hell to bring any proof that God is untrue. From the depths of hell I call the fiends, and from this earth I call the tried and afflicted believers, and to heaven I appeal, and challenge the long experience of the blood-washed host, and there is not to be found in the three realms a single person who can bear witness to one fact which can disprove the faithfulness of God, or weaken His claim to be trusted by His servants. There are many things that may or may not happen, but this I know *shall* happen—

> He *shall* present my soul,
>   Unblemish'd and complete,
> Before the glory of His face,
>   With joys divinely great.

All the purposes of man have been defeated, but not the purposes of God. The promises of man may be broken—many of them are made to be broken—but the promises of God shall all be fulfilled. He is a promise-maker, but He never was a promise-breaker; He is a promise-keeping God, and every one of His people shall prove it to be so. This is my grateful, personal confidence, "The

Lord *will* perfect that which concerneth *me*"—unworthy *me*, lost and ruined *me*. He will yet save *me;* and—

> I, among the blood-wash'd throng,
> Shall wave the palm, and wear the crown,
> And shout loud victory.

I go to a land which the plough of earth hath never upturned, where it is greener than earth's best pastures, and richer than her most abundant harvests ever saw. I go to a building of more gorgeous architecture than man hath ever builded; it is not of mortal design; it is "a building of God, a house not made with hands, eternal in the heavens." All I shall know and enjoy in heaven, will be given to me by the Lord, and I shall say, when at last I appear before Him—

> Grace all the work shall crown
> Through everlasting days;
> It lays in Heaven the topmost stone,
> And well deserves the praise.

## Christ's Sufficient Work

I know there are some who think it necessary to their system of theology to limit the merit of the blood of Jesus: if my theological system needed such a limitation, I would cast it to the winds. I cannot, I dare not allow the thought to find a lodging in my mind, it seems so near akin to blasphemy. In Christ's finished work I see an ocean of merit; my plummet finds no bottom, my eye discovers no shore. There must be sufficient efficacy in the blood of Christ, if God had so willed it, to have saved not only all in this world, but all in ten thousand worlds, had they transgressed their Maker's law. Once admit infinity into the matter, and limit is out of the question. Having a divine person for an offering, it is not consistent to conceive of limited value; bound and measure are terms inapplicable to the divine sacrifice. The intent of the divine purpose fixes the *application* of the infinite offering, but does not change it into a finite work.

Think of the numbers upon whom God has bestowed His grace already. Think of the countless hosts in Heaven: if thou wert introduced there to-day, thou wouldst find it as easy to tell the stars, or the sands of the sea, as to count the multitudes that are before the throne even now. They have come from the East, and from the West, from the North, and from the South, and they are sitting down with Abraham, and with Isaac, and with Jacob in the Kingdom of God; and beside those in heaven, think of the saved ones on earth. Blessed be God, His elect on earth are to be counted by millions, I believe, and the days are coming, brighter days than these, when there shall be multitudes upon multitudes brought to know the Savior, and to rejoice in Him.

The Father's love is not for a few only, but for an exceeding great company. "A great multitude, which no man could number," will be found in heaven. A man can reckon up to very high figures; set to work your Newtons, your mightiest calculators, and they can count great numbers, but God and God alone can tell the multitude of His redeemed. I believe there will be more in heaven than in hell. If anyone asks me why I think so, I answer, because Christ, in everything, is to "have the pre-eminence," and I cannot conceive how He could have the pre-eminence if there are to be more in the dominions of Satan than in paradise. Moreover, I have never read that there is to be in hell a great multitude, which no man could number. I rejoice to know that the souls of all infants, as soon as they die, speed their way to paradise. Think what a multitude there is of them! Then there are already in heaven unnumbered myriads of the spirits of just men made perfect—the redeemed of all nations, and kindreds, and people, and tongues up till now; and there are better times coming, when the religion of Christ shall be universal; when—

> He shall reign from pole to pole,
> With illimitable sway;

when whole kingdoms shall bow down before Him, and nations shall be born in a day, and in the thousand years of the great millennial state there will be enough saved to make up all the deficiencies of the thousands of years that have gone before. Christ shall be Master everywhere, and His praise shall be sounded in every land. Christ shall have the pre-eminence at last; His train shall be far larger than that which shall attend the chariot of the grim monarch of hell.

## Christ's Limited Atonement

Some persons love the doctrine of universal atonement because they say, "It is so beautiful. It is a lovely idea that Christ should have died for all men; it commends itself," they say, "to the instincts of humanity; there is something in it full of joy and beauty." I admit there is, but beauty may be often associated with falsehood. There is much which I might admire in the theory of universal redemption, but I will just show what the supposition necessarily involves. If Christ on His cross intended to save every man, then He intended to save those who were lost before He died. If the doctrine be true, that He died for all men, then He died for some who were in hell before He came into this world, for doubtless there were even then myriads there who had been cast away because of their sins.

Once again, if it was Christ's intention to save all men, how deplorably has He been disappointed, for we have His own testimony that there is a lake which burneth with fire and brimstone, and into that pit of woe have been cast some of the very persons who, according to the theory of universal redemption, were bought with His blood. That seems to me a conception a thousand times more repulsive than any of those consequences which are said to be associated with the Calvinistic and Christian doctrine of special and particular redemption. To think that my Savior died for men who were or are in hell, seems a supposition too horrible for me to entertain. To imagine for a moment that He was the Substitute for all the sons of men, and that God, having first punished the Substitute, afterwards punished the sinners themselves, seems to conflict with all my ideas of divine justice. That Christ should offer an atonement and satisfaction for the sins of all men, and that afterwards some of those very men should be punished for the sins for which Christ had already atoned, appears to me to be the most monstrous iniquity that could ever have been imputed to Saturn, to Janus, to the goddess of the Thugs, or to the most diabolical heathen deities. God forbid that we should ever think thus of Jehovah, the just and wise and good!

There is no soul living who holds more firmly to the doctrines of grace than I do, and if any man asks me whether I am ashamed to be called a Calvinist, I answer—I wish to be called nothing but a Christian; but if you ask me, do I hold the doctrinal views which were held by John Calvin, I reply, I do in the main hold them, and rejoice to avow it. But far be it from me even to imagine that Zion contains none but Calvinistic Christians within her walls, or that there are none saved who do not hold our views. Most atrocious things have been spoken about the character and spiritual condition of John Wesley, the modern prince of Arminians. I can only say concerning him that, while I detest many of the doctrines which he preached, yet for the man himself I have a reverence second to no Wesleyan; and if there were wanted two apostles to be added to the number of the twelve, I do not believe that there could be found two men more fit to be so added than George Whitefield and John Wesley. The character of John Wesley stands beyond all imputation for self-sacrifice, zeal, holiness, and communion with God; he lived far above the ordinary level of common Christians, and was one "of whom the world was not worthy." I believe there are multitudes of men who cannot see these truths, or, at least, cannot see them in the way in which we put them, who nevertheless have received Christ as their Savior, and are as dear to the heart of the God of grace as the soundest Calvinist in or out of heaven.

## The Problem with Hyper-Calvinism

I do not think I differ from any of my Hyper-Calvinistic brethren in what I do believe, but I differ from them in what they do not believe. I do not hold any less than they do, but I hold a little more, and, I think, a little more of the truth revealed in the Scriptures. Not only are there a few cardinal doctrines, by which we can steer our ship North, South, East, or West, but as we study the Word, we shall begin to learn something about the North-west and North-east, and all else that lies between the four cardinal points. The system of truth revealed in the Scriptures is not simply one straight line, but two; and no man will ever get a right view of the gospel until he knows how to look at the two lines at once.

For instance, I read in one Book of the Bible, "The Spirit and the bride say, Come. And let him that heareth say, Come. And let him that is athirst come. And whosoever will, let him take the water of life freely." Yet I am taught, in another part of the same inspired Word, that "it is not of him that willeth, nor of him that runneth, but of God that sheweth mercy." I see, in one place, God in providence presiding over all, and yet I see, and I cannot help seeing, that man acts as he pleases, and that God has left his actions, in a great measure, to his own free-will. Now, if I were to declare that man was so free to act that there was no control of God over his actions, I should be driven very near to atheism; and if, on the other hand, I should declare that God so over-rules all things that man is not free enough to be responsible, I should be driven at once into antinomianism or fatalism.

That God predestines, and yet that man is responsible, are two facts that few can see clearly. They are believed to be inconsistent and contradictory, but they are not. The fault is in our weak judgment. Two truths cannot be contradictory to each other. If, then, I find taught in one part of the Bible that everything is fore-ordained, *that is true;* and if I find, in another Scripture, that man is responsible for all his actions, *that is true;* and it is only my folly that leads me to imagine that these two truths can ever contradict each other. I do not believe they can ever be welded into one upon any earthly anvil, but they certainly shall be one in eternity. They are two lines that are so nearly parallel, that the human mind which pursues them farthest will never discover that they converge, but they do converge, and they will meet somewhere in eternity, close to the throne of God, whence all truth doth spring.

## The Doctrine of God's Grace Preserves Us from Sin

It is often said that the doctrines we believe have a tendency to lead us to sin. I have heard it asserted most positively, that those high doctrines which we love, and which we find in the Scriptures, are licentious ones. I do not know who will have the hardihood to make that assertion, when they consider that the holiest of men have been believers in them. I ask the man who dares to say that Calvinism is a licentious religion, what he thinks of the character of Augustine, or Calvin, or Whitefield, who in successive ages were the great exponents of the system of grace; or what will he say of the Puritans, whose works are full of them? Had a man been an Arminian in those days, he would have been accounted the vilest heretic breathing, but now *we* are looked upon as the heretics, and they as the orthodox. *We* have gone back to the old school; *we* can trace our descent from the apostles. It is that vein of free-grace, running through the sermonizing of Baptists, which has saved us as a denomination. Were it not for that, we should not stand where we are today. We can run a golden line up to Jesus Christ Himself, through a holy succession of mighty fathers, who all held these glorious truths; and we can ask concerning them, "Where will you find holier and better men in the world?"

No doctrine is so calculated to preserve a man from sin as the doctrine of the grace of God. Those who have called it "a licentious doctrine" did not know anything at all about it. Poor ignorant things, they little knew that their own vile stuff was the most licentious doctrine under heaven. If they knew the grace of God in truth, they would soon see that there was no preservative from lying like a knowledge that we are elect of God from the foundation of the world. There is nothing like a belief in my eternal perseverance, and the immutability of my Father's affection, which can keep me near to Him from a motive of simple gratitude. Nothing makes a man so virtuous as belief of the truth. A lying doctrine will soon beget a lying practice. A man cannot have an erroneous belief without by-and-by having an erroneous life. I believe the one thing naturally begets the other. Of all men, those have the most disinterested piety, the sublimest reverence, the most ardent devotion, who believe that they are saved by grace, without works, through faith, and that not of themselves, it is the gift of God. Christians should take heed, and see that it always is so, lest by any means Christ should be crucified afresh, and put to an open shame.

*"On Religious Grumblers" shows a witty and folksy side of Spurgeon that one does not immediately associate with his name. It is taken from an 1868 work titled* John Ploughman's Talk, *a work in which Spurgeon discards his usual manner of speech for "strong proverbial expressions and homely phrases" that he might reach the common man he was always most interested in. "That I have written in a semi-humorous vein needs no apology," he writes in the preface, "since thereby sound moral teaching has gained a hearing from at least 300,000 persons. There is no particular virtue in being seriously unreadable."*

*Spurgeon chose the persona of John Ploughman to reach the common man but also because "Every minister has put his hand to the plough: and it is his business to break up the fallow ground." The character of John Ploughman was patterned partially after his grandfather.*

# CHAPTER THIRTEEN

## *On Religious Grumblers*

When a man has a particularly empty head he generally sets up for a great judge, especially in religion. None so wise as the man who knows nothing. His ignorance is the mother of his impudence, and the nurse of his obstinacy; and though he does not know B from a bull's foot, he settles matters as if all wisdom were at his fingers' ends—the Pope himself is not more infallible. Hear him talk after he has been at meeting and heard a sermon, and you will know how to pull a good man to pieces if you never knew it before. He sees faults where there are none, and if there be a few things amiss, he makes every mouse into an elephant. Although you might put all his wit into an egg-shell, he weighs the sermon in the balances of his conceit with all the airs of a bred-and-born Solomon, and if it be up to his standard, he lays on his praise with a trowel; but if it be not to his taste, he growls and barks and snaps at it like a dog at a hedgehog.

Wise men in this world are like trees in a hedge, there is only here and there one; and when these rare men talk together upon a discourse, it is good for the ears to hear them; but the bragging wiseacres I am speaking of are vainly puffed up by their fleshly minds, and their quibbling is as senseless as the cackle of geese on a common. Nothing comes out of a sack but what was in it, and as their bag is empty they shake nothing but wind out of it. It is very likely that neither ministers nor their sermons are perfect— the best garden may have a few weeds in it, the cleanest corn may have some chaff—but cavillers cavil at anything or nothing, and find fault for the sake of showing off their deep knowledge: sooner than let their tongues have a holiday, they would complain that the grass is not a nice shade of blue, and say that the sky would have looked neater if it had been whitewashed.

## Highflying Ignoramuses

One tribe of these Ishmaelites is made up of highflying ignoramuses who are very mighty about the doctrine of a sermon—here they are as decisive as sledge-hammers and as certain as death. He who knows nothing is confident in everything; hence they are bullheaded beyond measure. Every clock, and even the sundial, must be set according to their watches; and the slightest difference from their opinion proves a man to be rotten at heart. Venture to argue with them, and their little pot boils over in quick style; ask them for reason, and you might as well go to a sand-pit for sugar. They have bottled up the sea of truth, and carry it in their waistcoat pockets; they have measured heaven's line of grace, and have tied a knot in a string at the exact length of electing love; and as for the things which angels long to know, they have seen them all as boys see sights in a peepshow at our fair. Having sold their modesty and become wiser than their teachers, they ride a very high horse, and jump over all five-barred gates of Bible-texts which teach doctrines contrary to their notions.

When this mischief happens to good men, it is a great pity for such sweet pots of ointment to be spoiled by flies, yet one learns to bear with them just as I do with old Violet, for he is a rare horse, though he does set his ears back and throw out his legs at times. But there is a black bragging lot about, who are all sting and no honey; all whip and no hay; all grunt and no bacon. These do nothing but rail from morning to night at all who cannot see through their spectacles. If they would but mix up a handful of good living with all their bushels of bounce, it would be more bearable; but no, they don't care for such legality; men so sound as they are can't be expected to be good at anything else; they are the heavenly watch-dogs to guard the house of the Lord from those thieves and robbers who don't preach sound doctrine, and if they do worry the sheep, or steal a rabbit or two by the sly, who would have the heart to blame them?

The Lord's *dear* people, as they call themselves, have enough to do to keep their doctrine sound; and if their manners are cracked, who can wonder! no man can see to everything at once. These are the moles that want catching in many of our pastures, not for their own sakes, for there is not a sweet mouthful in them, but for the sake of the meadows which they spoil. I would not find half a fault with their doctrine, if it were not for their spirit; but vinegar is sweet to it, and crabs are figs in comparison. It must be very high doctrine that is too high for me, but I must have high experience and high practice with it, or it turns my stomach. However, I have said my say, and must leave the subject, or somebody will ask me, "What have you to do with Bradshaw's windmill?"

## The Poor Trade of Judging Preachers

Sometimes it is the way the preacher speaks which is hauled over the coals, and here again is a fine field for fault hunting, for every bean has its black, and every man has his failing. I never knew a good horse which had not some odd habit or other, and I never yet saw a minister worth his salt who had not some crotchet or oddity: now, these are the bits of cheese which cavillers smell out and nibble at: this man is too slow, and another too fast; the first is too flowery, and the second is too dull. Dear me, if all God's creatures were judged in this way, we should wring the dove's neck for being too tame, shoot the robins for eating spiders, kill the cows for swinging their tails, and the hens for not giving us milk. When a man wants to beat a dog, he can soon find a stick; and at this rate any fool may have something to say against the best minister in England.

As to a preacher's manner, if there be but plain speaking, none shall cavil at it because it wants polish, for if a thing is good and earnestly spoken, it cannot sound much amiss. No man should use bad language in the pulpit—and all language is bad which common people cannot make head or tail of—but godly, sober, decent, plain words none should carp at. A countryman is as warm in fustian as a king in velvet, and a truth is as comfortable in homely words as in fine speech. As to the way of dishing up the meat, hungry men leave that to the cook, only let the meat be sweet and substantial.

If hearers were better, sermons would be better. When

men say they can't hear, I recommend them to buy a horn, and remember the old saying, "There's none so deaf as those who will not hear." When young speakers get down-hearted because of hard, unkind remarks, I generally tell them of the old man and his boy and his ass, and what came of trying to please everybody. No piper ever suited all ears. Where whims and fancies sit in the seat of judgment, a man's opinion is only so much wind, therefore take no more notice of it than of the wind whistling through a keyhole.

I have heard men find fault with a discourse for what was not in it; no matter how well the subject in hand was brought out, there was another subject about which nothing was said, and so all was wrong; which is as reasonable as finding fault with my ploughing because it does not dibble the holes for the beans, or abusing a good corn-field because there are no turnips in it. Does any man look for every truth in one sermon? As well look for every dish at one meal, and rail at a joint of beef because there are neither bacon, nor veal, nor green peas, nor parsnips on the table. Suppose a sermon is not full of comfort to the saint, yet if it warn the sinner, shall we despise it? A handsaw would be a poor tool to shave with, shall we therefore throw it away? Where is the use of always trying to hunt out faults? I hate to see a man with a fine nose smelling about for things to rail at like a rat-catcher's dog sniffing at rat holes. By all means let us down with error, root and branch, but do let us save our billhooks till there are brambles to chop, and not fall foul of our own mercies.

Judging preachers is a poor trade, for it pays neither party concerned in it. At a ploughing match they do give a prize to the best of us; but these judges of preaching are precious slow to give anything even to those whom they profess to think so much of. They pay in praise, but give no pudding. They get the gospel for nothing, and if they do not grumble, think that they have made an abundant return.

Everybody thinks himself a judge of a sermon, but nine out of ten might as well pretend to weigh the moon. I believe that, at bottom, most people think it an uncommonly easy thing to preach, and that they could do it amazingly well themselves. Every donkey thinks itself worthy to stand with the king's horses; every girl thinks she could keep house better than her mother; but thoughts are not facts; for the sprat thought itself a herring, but the fisherman knew better.

I dare say those who can whistle fancy that they can plough; but there's more than whistling in a good ploughman, and so let me tell you there's more in good preaching than taking a text, and saying, firstly, secondly, and thirdly. I try my hand at preaching myself, and in my poor way I find it no very easy thing to give the folks something worth hearing; and if the fine critics, who reckon us up on their thumbs, would but try their own hands at it, they might be a little more quiet. Dogs, however, always will bark, and what is worse, some of them will bite too; but let decent people do all they can, if not to muzzle them, yet to prevent them doing any great mischief.

## Fault-Finders

It is a dreadful thing to see a happy family of Christians broken up by talkative fault-finders, and all about nothing, or less than nothing. Small is the edge of the wedge, but when the devil handles the beetle, churches are soon split to pieces, and men wonder why. The fact is, the worst wheel of the cart creaks most, and one fool makes many, and thus many a congregation is set at ears with a good and faithful minister, who would have been a lasting blessing to them if they had not chased away their best friend. Those who are at the bottom of the mischief have generally no part or lot in the matter of true godliness, but, like sparrows, fight over corn which is not their own, and, like jackdaws, pull to pieces what they never helped to build. From mad dogs, and grumbling professors, may we all be delivered, and may we never take the complaint from either of them.

Fault-finding is dreadfully catching: one dog will set a whole kennel howling, and the wisest course is to keep out of the way of a man who has the complaint called the grumbles. The worst of it is, that the foot and mouth disease go together, and he who bespatters others generally rolls in the mud himself before long. "The fruit of the Spirit is love," and this is a very different apple from the sour Siberian crab which some people bring forth. Good bye, all ye sons of Grizzle, John Ploughman would sooner pick a bone in peace than fight over an ox roasted whole.